God, Bible
And Country

David L. Mundine

God, Bible And Country

By David L. Mundine

Published By
Positive Imaging, LLC
9016 Palace Parkway
Austin, TX 78748
bill@positive-imaging.com

Cover Art by Jeanie Brooks-Mundine

All Rights Reserved

No part of this publication may be reproduced in whole or in part, or stored in a retrieval system, or transmitted in any form or by any means, electronic, mechanical, printing, photocopying, recording or otherwise without written permission from the publisher, except for the inclusion of brief quotations in a review. For information regarding permission, contact the publisher.

Copyright   2019   David L. Mundine

ISBN 9781951776008

Dedication

While writing this book I lost four of the most important and influential people in my life. I lost my father, a godly man whose incredible love for his family gave me inspiration and encouragement throughout life's journey. My best friend for forty-five years, Jim, who stood diligently by my side and was always a great source of strength and support. He and I shared an incredible journey of friendship.

And then my friends Amos and Clara Grace were huge influences in my youth; I cherish the memories of these ~ special ones in my life. I miss them all so much.

And always to my wife, Jeanie for her love and support.

Acknowledgments

A special thank you to my publisher, Bill Benitez who owns Positive Imaging, LLC., for his patience and guidance.

And one more special thank you to my patient wife, Jeanie for her long hours of typing and editing.

David lives with his wife, Jeanie, their faithful old dog, Polly, and two cats, Tiger and Noelle in beautiful central Texas. When not writing or studying the Bible, they enjoy travelling and seeing all the beautiful sights of our great nation. They both enjoy church and attend regularly giving God the praise He so rightfully deserves, and spending time with their church family.

David has a deep love for studying history and has done so his entire life. He felt he must share his concerns in regard to the troubling course America is on today. The American Dream and Christian values as a whole are under attack from enemies within. Many good Christians share my concerns and love for our great nation. Therefore, every Christian must wake up and stand up and defend our religious liberties lest they be taken away. America is under attack my friends and fellow Christians, so we must fight the good fight for God and country.

Ephesians 6: 11 "Put on the full armour of God, so that you can take your stand against the devil's schemes." NIV

"Put on the whole armour of God, that ye may be able to stand against the wiles of the devil." KJV

Contents

Author's Remarks 11
Foreword 13
Introduction 15
Part One 17
  Chapter One 19
  Chapter Two 23
  Chapter Three 25
  Chapter Four 29
  Chapter Five 33
  Chapter Six 35
  Chapter Seven 39
  Chapter Eight 41
  Chapter Nine 43
  Chapter Ten 45
  Chapter Eleven 49
Part Two 55
  Great Leaders 56
    Oral Roberts 57
    William Franklin Graham, Jr. 63
    Martin Luther King, Jr. 71
  False Leaders 79
    Jim Jones 81
    Marshall Herff Applewhite 85
    David Koresh 87

Part Three   91
     English Poet John Newton   93
     Poet William Cowper   95
     Pastor Thomas Dorsey   97
     Poet Henry Wadworth Longfellow   99

Part Four   101
     Testimony   103
     Stand Up For God   111
     Stand Up For Christ   113
     A Good, Though Misguided Friend   115

Part Five   117
     Job   119
     Lazarus   123
     Paul   129
     Moses   135
     Pharisees   139
     Prophets   141

Part Six   145
     Jesus   147
     Who Do You Say I Am?   151
     Jesus Preaching   155
     Jesus Teaching   159
     Jesus Man Of Myth   161
     Doubt and Disciples   165
     So Who Is The Holy Spirit   169
     Holy Spirit   171
     Is The Devil Real   175
     Seeker of Truth   177

Jesus And Woman	179
Jesus And Children	181
Part Seven	183
Jesus and Enemies	185
Enemy Of God	189
Repent From Sin	191
Part Eight	193
Second Coming	195
Land Of Jesus	199
Death and After	203
Closing	207

Author's Remarks

How fondly I remember growing up in the small central Texas town of Lexington, population 611; seems as if that number stayed on the city limits sign for decades. Lexington was so small there was not one traffic light, not even out on the highway, let alone in the town itself, in fact she just received her first blinking light in recent years. Now I am a lifetime away from the placid fifties era in which I was raised. But, the fifties were just a perfect time to have grown up in, it was such an innocent time period. Lexington, Texas was our Mayberry, and it felt to me as if we lived with all those characters from the popular fifties television series, "The Andy Griffith Show", as indeed we had our Andys, and our Barneys, and yes, we even had a few Otis's, Ernest T.'s and Gomers, as well, and there was no shortage of Aunt Bea's, either. Those of us fortunate enough to have been raised in this more kinder, gentler time in our country know how blessed we are. As a youth in this idyllic community, and had I been able to see more deeply into our country's future I am sure I would have appreciated the present much more. Therein lies the truth of the old adage, "hindsight's twenty twenty", so very true. From 1946 to 1964 the US birthrate spiked to almost seventy eight million and thusly became known as the Baby Boom Era.

Churches were filled with wide-awake Christians hungry for the Word of God. After World War II, tent revivals abounded in almost every town from coast to coast, our nation's faith was at a charismatic level. Radios broadcasted religious programs into peoples' homes providing the Gospel with the mere twist of a knob and gave great comfort as folks gathered around the device that brought the world into their homes. The mid 1950's was about to bring a change to religion forever because evangelism over the airwaves had begun. In a few years, what with the invention of television and with more and more homes acquiring a tv set, the televangelism era began. This new way of hearing God's Word took root and would play a significant role in America's religious experience. You will be reading about some of those great preachers and to be fair, you will also read about some leaders who abused their privilege and power. With this being said, I hope you will enjoy the reading of God, Bible, and Country.

Foreword

For everyone out there who has ever thought, I should write a book ... yes, maybe you should. I have twice now and I must tell you it is a very liberating, though somewhat grueling process. It was for me, anyway, because I have no filter at times, and tend to write whatever springs into my mind and then have the arduous task of stringing it together to try and make sense for my readers so that you will actually benefit from my words. So look, this book is part personal journal, part biblical history, part American history, and part world history. As I look around at the nation and the world and see the absolute hatred being spewed out at every opportunity, it simply grieves me because I know this is not what our heavenly Father wants for us nor expects from us. People, we need to pull the wagon together or we are going to self destruct this entire nation and the world as we know it. I write because these things weigh heavily on my heart every day and I feel as if I will burst wide open if I do not say something. Some of my writings may seem like rantings or tangents, but I can assure you this is not the case. My hope is that you will feel as if I am just really having a conversation with you, that you are just sitting here listening to my musings and hopefully hearing a modicum of my so-called wit and wisdom. After all, when we converse together don't we tend to go off on different subjects and then return to the one we began with? When you read this book, please consider it as having a conversation with me, albeit one-sided since you cannot talk back, but if it sets you to thinking, then I have accomplished what I set out to do. Also, understanding this, then maybe you won't be so concerned with the "flow" of the words and ideas but rather more attentive to the content. The main idea of the following chapters is for you to get involved with your Lord, which is what God placed us here for in the first place. We are each given a certain amount of time in which to accomplish the purpose God created us for. To love Him, to love one another, and to attain eternal life. May you be richly blessed and rest in the knowledge that our God is greater than anything in this world. Remember that if you don't like something, change it. It is easy to tear something down, but God wants us to pray for our leaders, and build them up rather than wish for them to be destroyed. Do something. Vote. Get involved. And always, always Love. Love God. Love yourselves. Love one another. And don't worry about anything. God has this.

Phillippians 4:6-7 do not be anxious about anything, but in everything by prayer and supplication with thanksgiving let your requests be made known to God.

"Worry is interest paid on trouble before it comes due."
~ Dean Inge 1932

Introduction

Between the covers of this book, you will find interesting stories of different individuals throughout history, from the time of Jesus to the present time. Fascinating stories of people in scripture who walked with Jesus and came to love him. You will understand how our brave and courageous forefathers, with their faith in God, built the greatest nation on Earth.

In the coming pages you will find accounts of heroes and villains, and of great leaders and false leaders, as this book will confront some of today's difficult issues, issues that some Christians try to avoid.

Today, Christians must wake up and take a conscious look at America's new identity. Our nation is now divided and has become a nation of anxiety. Our politicians and their constituency are full of hatred and rage. The future of America rests in the hands of the Christian voters. I believe that right now there is still a great hunger of mind and a thirst of soul within ordinary men and women to look for a true peace with God. It is my prayer that you will be filled with hunger and thirst to search for God if you haven't yet found Him, and to be edified and restored if you are already a Christian believer.

Prayerfully, I hope your hunger and thirst are met herein.

David Mundine

God, Bible
And Country

Part One

1

Brave American founders made a covenant with God wherein they promised their love and loyalty to God and consequently built the most beautiful and powerful nation the world has ever seen. Our founding fathers had a tremendous vision of what America should become. They pledged their loyalty and lives to build a nation made for God-loving Christians. John Adams spoke proudly of our constitution, a constitution that was made only for a moral and religious people. It is wholly inadequate to the government of any other. I love America, but I am always a Christian first and an American second. I do not embrace or share any loyalty to any political party. When I vote, I ask myself one question: If Jesus was casting his ballot in the voting booth beside me, whom would he choose? Whom would he vote for? And then I choose my vote with my faith. The signers of the Declaration of Independence, John Hancock and John Adams signed, "We recognize no sovereign but God and no king but Jesus!" In 2017 President Donald Trump told the crowd at the Values Voter Summit in Washington, DC, *"In America we don't worship government - we worship God!"*

I still believe in America and I am not ready to throw in the towel because this great nation still has a pulse, so let's not be ready to write her obituary. There is still hope for our beloved nation, and as soon as Christian's wake up in their pews and wipe the fog of slumber from their tired, blind eyes and see America with freshly awakened spiritual eyes, then they may go to the polls and start voting for good people who embrace Christ and will lead America back to its moral pathway. Vote for those who support traditional family values and hate evil. The balance of America's future rests in the hands of Christian voters. The Christian vote can determine the future course of America.

Revelation 3:2-3 *"Wake up! Strengthen what remains and is about to die, for I have not found your deeds complete in the sight of God. Remember, therefore, what you have received and heard. Obey it, and repent. But if you do not wake up, I will come like a thief, you will not know at what time I will come against you."*

Patriot Samuel Adams spoke of the importance and trust of every vote. *"Let each citizen remember at the moment he is offering his vote that he is not making a present or a compliment to please an individual or at least that he ought not to do so. But that he is executing one of the most solemn trusts in human society for which he is accountable to God and his country."*

Romans 13:1-2 *"there is no government anywhere that God has not placed in power"... "So those who refuse to obey God, punishment will follow."*

God told Moses how to choose good leaders: Exodus 18:21 *"Choose Godly, honest men who hate bribes, appoint them as judges, select men who fear God."*

Proverbs 22:3 *"A prudent man foresees the difficulties ahead and prepares for them; the simpleton goes blindly on and suffers the consequences."*

Chapter One

Matthew 26:40 (Sleeping through a crisis) - *"Could ye not watch with me one hour?*

2

The United States of America, despite all its problems, is still the sole superpower of our planet. We are still *"One Nation Under God"*. Our currency still reads, *"In God We Trust"*. We still are *"The Land of The Free and The Home of The Brave"*. There is absolutely no doubt America is a mighty nation. God has blessed America for almost two and a half centuries, she is blessed with beautiful cities located on many different water ports that bring great wealth to our nation from a jealous world. America is 4% of the world's population yet controls more than 20% of the world's total gross domestic product. We are a nation of luxurious wealth. Most importantly America is a solid Christian nation where more than 90% of the adult population claim to be believers of Christ. Man can determine his future by the character of his choices. We are divinely created in the image of our Father God. God has granted us the ability to make conscious choices in our lives, we are granted the ability to make deliberate decisions choosing to be honest or dishonest. The worth and dignity of man is his faith in God. Ask yourself how deep is your faith? Can it withstand the storms and the adversities of life? How sadly I fear our nation has clearly changed, just in the past ten years. It is my feeling our beautiful nation is being threatened from within by its own people as we are no longer a united nation, but rather we are acting as a divided nation. We have strayed from the path God wants us to be on and we have chosen leaders who have caused much harm to our beautiful nation. Weak leadership has tarnished and divided our nation.

Going back in history, President Abraham Lincoln clearly understood the importance of a united nation and the tragedy of a divided nation when he spoke about America. He said that America would never be destroyed from outside forces, that if we should ever lose our freedom it would be because we faltered and destroyed ourselves. Brave leader Abraham Lincoln understood the power and importance of following the true word of God as in the Bible. Lincoln was right when he said God's best gift to man is the Bible. The very foundation of our great nation is based upon moral and religious people. Our courageous founding fathers pledged their lives and sacred honor for America and marched forward with God's blessings to build the mightiest nation the world has ever seen. President John Adams spoke about our Constitution saying, *"Our Constitution was made only for a moral and religious people. It is wholly inadequate to the government of any other."*

In 1801 Thomas Jefferson wrote a letter to close friend John Dickinson expressing deep concerns about our nation's two parties, Republicans and Federalists. In his letter he stated, "My dear friend if we do not find a way to satisfy small differences of opinion we can never act together, every man cannot have his way. In all, the greatest good we can do *our* country *is* to heal our party divisions and make them one people".

3

I have struggled for months about addressing some of the difficult issues on the next pages, understanding fully that some of you reading this will find certain of the following issues I will discuss troubling and disturbing. These are things weighing on my heart and mind and as a Christian I feel it is wrong to see evil and not call it by its name. To do nothing is to condone wrong thinking [actions] and I do not. Honestly, I seek no joy or pleasure in saying unflattering things about others. Though I am human and I cannot help myself when I become offended by another person calling me a deplorable or when a President (and others in the public eye), mocks and ridicules my Christian faith as has happened in the past. So please read on knowing that I am going to speak my piece about our nation, our world and our religion. We cannot help but ask ourselves what lies ahead for our America. What does our future hold? What is the next event and sign of Jesus' return? These questions are on the minds of Christians everywhere, and if they are not they should be. The disturbing tide of sin is so great, can any of us doubt that we are living in the last days? Though no one knows, not even the angels in Heaven, when that time will be, we collectively feel it is coming sooner rather than later. The work of the Antichrist can plainly be seen and heard. Is our world finally coming to a climax because many totally reject God? Is our world coming to a final judgment like the days of Noah? Prophecy is history written in advance. What God's prophets have written will take place. The Bible adequately explains our nation's and our world's future. Over and over again God has promised that He is coming. And many fiercely-faithful and spirit-filled believers are watching and waiting. But the Antichrist will appear and pretend to care about the world's problems and dilemmas experienced each day. And he will appear to be the world-savior, but he is a lie, as the world will discover that he is the Antichrist of written prophecy, the beast from Hell in the form of a man. Our very eyes are seeing everywhere some of the definite signs of the last days. The big question looming over us is how close are we to the coming of Christ? The number one sign of Christ's return is when Jews who have been scattered all over the world begin returning to Israel. The eyes of all Jews will be opened and see clearer than ever before and they will believe and accept that Jesus Christ is the Messiah and true Son of God. The Bible urges people to prepare and clean up their lives, separating themselves from this present evil and wicked world. Jesus promised us there shall be upon Earth distress of nations. Prophecies tell us man will witness in end times a huge increase in travel and knowledge. This is evident in our vast leaps in technologies, with having the world at our fingertips. What with our computers, cell phones, televisions, and satellites circling the globe bringing live reports of happenings around the world. In effect, making the entire world and its goings on accessible to anyone with these forms of technology. And though some do not have these devices readily available, this too, is becoming more and more prevalent. God is stirring the hearts of missionaries in foreign lands to preach repentance for deliverance as it is God's desire for all people to come together for the final revival of Christ. All Americans are greatly indebted to our brave Pilgrim forefathers whose visions and

Chapter Three

desires it was to worship God with full liberty. We must protect our religious freedoms, and we must read and understand our Bibles, for our Bible is God's forecast of the future, it will reveal the fascinating events that shall come to pass.

4

Today Americans live under two sets of laws; the laws of God and the laws of Man; many of us are placing man's laws above those of God. The danger in doing this is that man made laws are often flawed and some are even immoral. God's laws are always the truth and lead to everlasting life with Jesus Christ. If we violate man's law we may go to jail, but if we violate God's laws we will go to a much warmer place! When we disobey God we are literally playing with fire. God's laws should always come first in our lives. Never place an idol or law above those of God. All God-fearing Christian people should fight any evil forces that try to separate them from God. Sorrowfully, there are people with few if any, moral restraints, and who place man's laws above God's laws and adopt an almost anything goes attitude, thinking if it feels good, and fits my lifestyle let's go for it! Silence when we see evil is in itself evil. People must speak up and call out evil acts and put them in the light because evil cannot live in the light, it will always die for sin can only live in absolute darkness. Every Christian has a moral obligation to wake up and make a moral impact for society, the time is now to fight the good fight. We have been asleep and silent far too long, people, it is time to strengthen what remains. Today's new democratic party is not the same party it was a decade ago. Not your momma's (or your father's) party anymore! It has today taken on a totally new identity and what remains seems only a shadow of what it once was. The Democratic Party has turned into an angry mob with no moral compass nor agenda, they have fallen away from God. The new ideals they embrace so vehemently are not Christian nor American. Instead they have become the party of pure hate and resistance, waging war on Christian values. Democrats are so intoxicated by hatred that they no longer care for the security of American citizens. Their behavior is non-redeemable because they so stubbornly resist and refuse to work on solving problems, seeking only to tear down that which America was built upon. Our core values are on the chopping block and many of us sit back and watch as it happens. Is this your Democratic Party? Ask yourselves if this is the new American Dream:

>   Late term abortion
>   Socialism
>   Open borders with revolving doors
>   Welfare dependency
>   High taxation
>   22 Trillion dollar national debt
>   Devalued traditional marriage

The new Democratic Party is saturated with an all-absorbing, raging hatred and unhinged stupidity. Will you let them disrespect God and wreak havoc on America with their Marxist agendas?

Luke 11:23 *"Anyone who is not for me is against me; if he isn t helping me, he is hurting my cause."*

Matthew 12:30 *"Anyone who isn't helping me is harming me."*

We must restore and protect our religious liberties and protect our freedom of speech. We must recognize no

Chapter Four

sovereign but God, and no king but Jesus. We must fight for our Christian future and again become a solid influence in public life. We must stop the corrosion of America and The American Dream. America was built on hard work and a Christian spirit, it was not built to become a nation for the liberal indoctrination of socialism. Brave patriots pledged their very lives and honor to build the mightiest nation on Earth. These brave men would never stand by and let a political party have power to destroy what the great people of God built. Wake up! And stand for God and Nation! **America's future rests in the hands of Christian voters.**

In February 2019 the Harris Poll told us that 50% of Millenials prefer living in a socialist nation. Obviously, those people have never lived in a socialist nation and endured a life of misery. Today many of our radical left college professors are brainwashing our youth into thinking everything in America should be FREE and hard work is no longer necessary. Well, just look around at how that's been working out. Socialism only benefits those who are lazy and have low self-esteem. Socialism kills the American Dream and always leads to tyranny and oppression. In 2011 Venezuela was the richest country in South America, sitting on an ocean of oil. They chose to embrace socialism and now you can see them searching for food scraps in trash cans and eating out of the backs of garbage trucks, scrounging for food so starving are they. Ask any Historian and you will be told that massive evidence proves Socialism always fails. It only leads to oppression in its severest form. Ask yourself if you are willing to give up the American Dream that has made America the most powerful nation on Earth for almost 250 years, in order to embrace failed socialist ideas. Ask yourself if you are willing to change America from a sovereign constitutional republic to a socialist democracy. America was founded by brave Christians to be a proud and godly and free society. America was built by hardworking Christians. Are you so willing to give this up? I certainly am not. One of the driving forces for me to write this book is to try and wake up my fellow citizens, to wake up Americans to what is going on around us, and to plead with everyone to sit up and take notice, take action when and where you can, and bring America back to the land of the free by loving and respecting our God, our flag and our country.

5

America is still the greatest nation on Earth and God has blessed her in so many ways. We are the most generous nation when we see others in need of help. We are always among the first to feed the hungry and serve the poor and the oppressed of the world. As a Christian I cannot help being concerned for the future of our great nation. Tragically, America is becoming a divided nation with people arguing and fighting in our streets. Some are choosing sides and squabbling among themselves. We have also developed a huge drug problem. In 2017, seventy-two thousand Americans died from drug overdoses. Of those deaths, 68% involved Opioids - that number totals larger than all the American lives lost in the entire Vietnam War.

In the past seven years church attendance in American churches has dropped 7%. God has told us to watch and prepare for his coming. This is a time for us Americans to unite and step closer to God. The good news is that in other parts of the world millions are finding their way to Christ. In some of the most ungodly places, in some of the most unlikely places, a great revival is happening and millions are awakening and finding God in their lives. A great revival and awakening is going on around the world as people are seeking Christ and recognizing he is the Savior of our world. In China 48 million have given their lives to Christ, and in the next 50 years experts estimate that this number could easily triple over the next generation. For the first time in this communist nation's history, people are optimistic about the future because they no longer live in an empty void with an atheistic future looming and no hope of salvation. They have been released from the chains of bondage. The main reason for this great revival is the hard work of brave missionaries who bring the Gospel to places like China, Korea, Nigeria, and Argentina. The selfless acts of these many *missionaries* is making a huge difference in bringing souls to Christ, giving hope to the depressed, the oppressed, and the discouraged so the light of God may come into their hearts. Because of our missionaries a great harvest of Christianity is *exploding* around the world in formerly godless places and people are recognizing and accepting Christ.

6

I am *going* to *subtitle this chapter* "The *Bonnie and Clyde* of *Politics"* so *that when* you are reading this account you must remember these are my words and my opinions. But also keep in mind these words, [with the exception of my straight up opinions] are also factual.

On September 10, 2016 at a fundraiser rally in New York City pathological liar and presidential candidate, Hillary Clinton called Trump supporters <u>"A basket of deplorables"</u>. For decades Bill and Hillary Clinton have clearly earned the title of *"The Bonnie and Clyde of American Politics"*. These two so-called "partners in crime" have blazed a trail of crime and corruption from Little Rock, Arkansas to the White House in Washington, DC, leaving a trail of misery and destruction everywhere they have gone. Everyone involved with these two villains has the unwanted opportunity to become a scapegoat or a casualty as they seem to use people for speed bumps along their trail of corruption. Affiliated with them one may end up dead under mysterious circumstances or find oneself in prison with any dreams of a career shattered by these two "outlaws". They are shameless and blameless for decades' worth of dastardly, scandalous behavior. It is hard for me to believe these two people ever found one another and married because they have such totally different personalities. Bill Clinton is a very likeable man with such a charismatic personality; he is polite and has a way of making anyone around him feel comfortable. He is a tremendously smart man and is in fact a Rhodes Scholar. Some claim Bill can charm the birds out of the trees to eat from his hand while poor Hillary, with her type of personality could not even coach a starving cat to eat. As I see it, Bill's biggest downfall outside of being married to Hillary, is being oversexed. If having affairs and chasing younger women ever became an Olympic event, I would place all my money on Bill winning the Gold. That poor man just cannot help himself, he has the manners of an alley cat on the prowl overdosed on Viagra. In my humble opinion, of course.

Both Clintons admit no responsibility for their unethical, illegal behavior. There will never be any apology for their conduct, only denials. In 2014 Hillary's book, a memoir titled <u>Hard Choices</u> came out, wherein she painted herself as a crusading hero for America. The only "hard choices" Hillary ever made was trying to tell the truth and she failed miserably at it. One woman working on Hillary's campaign quit in the middle of it and said she could not take it anymore because Hillary is both truthless and soulless. Hillary has a volcanic temper that is easy to erupt, and she does not have enough good qualities to be President, lacking both the integrity and the temperament for any office let alone that required of the President of the United States.

In 2012 Ambassador Chris Stevens pleaded with the then U.S. Secretary of State Hillary Clinton for more Embassy security in Benghazi. Hillary failed to send more security and we all know how that turned out. Days later Ambassador Chris Stevens and three other men were tragically killed in the Benghazi attack. From the Whitewater fiasco to the Benghazi tragedy, and let me also include the questionable Clinton Foundation,

Chapter Six

the list of scandals goes on and on with no end in sight. And yet, people still defend these two partners in crime. It is amazing, only in America!

Yet, all the hundreds of millions of dollars Hillary spent on television ads could not buy her the White House. However, after the Presidential election she ran around crying how she was cheated out of that election. She blamed everyone but herself. The truth is that just enough good Christians were awake back then and voted to keep this arrogant, evil woman from destroying our America. **Voting for Hillary Clinton would make about as much sense as a chicken voting for Colonel Sanders!** Another of my humble opinions.

7

For eight long years I watched the radical, anti-Christian Obama administration poison and divide our beautiful nation. President Obama traveled to other nations and proudly announced to the world, America is no longer a Christian Nation! He told people that Christians love to hold a Bible in one hand and a gun in the other. Obama became our first President to refuse to acknowledge our National Day of Prayer which was started by President Harry S. Truman and the Reverend Billy Graham in the early 1950's. Obama shamefully apologized to other nations for America's behavior.

As soon as Obama became President he passed a bill called the Mexico City Policy. This new law would allow Christians' hard-earned tax monies to be spent on overseas abortions in poor third world countries. Obama disregarded our closest allies and rewarded our terrorist enemies with pallets of U.S. taxpayers' money as all the while those recipients shouted "death to America!", and burned and stomped our proud flag in their streets for the whole world to see. I watched this poor excuse of a leader mock and disrespect our Christian nation while he was in power and when he should have been leading our nation. No doubt he will easily go down in history as America's worst President.

8

On January 22, 2019 the pro-choice Democratic Party voted and passed into law a bill that allows abortions to be performed mere hours before natural birth would occur. When the bill passed this group of hyenas loudly celebrated and cheered and ran around the room high-fiving one another. You would have thought they had just won the superbowl the way they carried on, shamelessly celebrating the legal right to murder a child via abortion just hours before its' natural birth should occur. Not since Adolph Hitler has such a barbaric behavior been witnessed. In America 24% of babies conceived are executed in their mother's womb. More than 40% of New York City's pregnancies end in abortion; such grim statistics.

As previously stated, former President Barack Obama vigorously promoted overseas abortions by passing the (Mexico City Policy) that allowed American taxpayer money to support abortions there and in other poor nations. This shameful act influenced other nations to follow America's lead and allow abortions globally, resulting in more than one billion babies worldwide having been aborted. Evil President Obama let that be part of your legacy.

Ezekiel 36:18 *"They polluted the land with murder and with the worship of idols, so I poured out my fury upon them.*

Jeremiah 1:5 *"I knew you before you were formed within your mother's womb; before you were born I sanctified you and appointed you as my spokesman to the world.*

Thomas Jefferson spoke of God's judgment for America, *"I tremble for my country when I reflect that God is just; that his justice cannot sleep forever."*

The Reverend Billy Graham firmly believed life begins at conception and he often told others that he wanted to live to be a hundred years old. If you count the months he spent in his mother's womb, God blessed you, Billy, you made the one hundred year mark!

While listening to a television show one night, I heard a fellow relate a story about a man in deep grief who was on his knees praying to God. This man had just lost his wife of more than 50 years to cancer. He had also lost several close friends who had died of this dreadful disease. So he prayed to God to please send us [the world] someone to cure this terrible disease which is causing so much pain, suffering and death in our lives. God's voice came to him loud and clear from Heaven; *I have witnessed your pain and suffering, and I have sent you a research doctor and a scientist to cure and take away from you this horrific disease. And you, [mankind], you aborted both of them!* How many great doctors, scientists, teachers and leaders must we destroy before we come back to our senses and stop killing our most precious gifts from God? No one has the right to play God and determine who lives and dies.

Mike Huckabee, a former Governor of Arkansas said that, *"America is going to Hell in a hand basket if we*

9

Some will find this book very controversial because in it I am challenging the teachings that are being purported in today's modern church, challenging today's religious leaders and their new methods and the scripture-altering ways they are preaching and teaching the Holy Bible. I feel some leaders in today's churches have overlooked both biblical and historical facts and principles, even re-writing the Bible and misrepresenting scriptures to justify their sinful lifestyles. In the past 50 years or so some of our churches have changed; in fact, many of our churches have changed. Religious leaders continually ignore traditional teachings of the Bible and seem to purposefully avoid controversial issues, not wanting to be politically incorrect or hurt anyone's feelings. Hellfire and brimstone preaching has become a thing of the past, after all, we certainly wouldn't wish to offend anyone's sensitivity by reading and preaching the Bible as it was written. Since this kind of teaching might make folks uncomfortable, today's preachers are adapting a different gospel, one that has little resemblance to what our Heavenly Father has planned for mankind. Some church doctrines have compromised with Satan and are now allowing false leaders to preach. Apostle Paul warned his young disciple, Timothy, to look out for false leaders coming into the churches in end times. God tells us in scripture that He will never change, but unfortunately many of the followers of Christ have changed. It has been many years since I heard a preacher behind the pulpit shout boldly to his church members about sin and the eternal punishment of Hell. Today we assemble to hear a feel-good sermon from a motivational speaker rather than a preacher, wanting us to believe that God has changed, that the Holy Bible has become outdated. These folks are gravely mistaken because God is the same yesterday, today and forever. God has not changed. But we have. When Jesus preached, his ministry was bold and direct and to the point. He challenged the teachings of the Pharisees and called them hypocrites because they had abandoned the true tradition of scripture and perverted it with wickedness. Jesus told them Isaiah's prophecies were true and correct and that they [Pharisees] were just hypocrites. Jesus often told his disciples that his Father's primary concern was salvation for his children, saying that his Father would never give up on any of his children because of their sins. God's unfailing love can restore souls, cleansing them of their evilness, purifying even to newness that which is God's desire to save all of his children. Jesus' loving kindness and gentle mercies for all clearly showed his glory. Everyone around Jesus enjoyed a magnitude of mercy and love, and victory over sin and death. The Grace of God is stronger than any sin. God is always in complete control of mankind's destiny. God's love is eternal and everlasting, he is the good shepherd and his sheep hear his voice and follow him.

"Whoever eats my flesh and drinks my blood has eternal life: ~ John 6:54

10

All Christians today recognize the Bible as the most important book the world has ever known and scripture tells us how to live and how to love one another. The Bible can unlock the many mysteries about the rise and fall of great nations. Today many Bible prophecies are coming true before our eyes, clearly explaining present and future historic events. The Bible is the only history book in the world that can not only tell us of our past but it can also tell us facts concerning our future. Our Bible points to more than 3,856 verses directly or indirectly to prophecy in scripture. Many of these prophecies have proven to be incredible scientific facts. Many early-century Bible skeptics laughed at Bible predictions in ancient times. Today these scriptural predictions are becoming fulfilled giving credibility to the Bible for all of us including those naysayers. Almost four thousand years ago predictions forecasted the whole Middle East conflict and promised much destruction to come. Ancient Bible scriptures foretold of the destruction of Jerusalem and the scattering of the Jewish people throughout the world. Predicting the rebirth of Israel in one day, on May 14, 1948 Britain signed papers that gave back the land promised by God to His Jewish people. In Isaiah 66:7 (700 BC) *"Before she travailed, she brought forth; before her pain came, she was delivered of a man child."* Prophet Isaiah gives us one of our most powerful and accurate prophecies. Who has heard or seen anything as strange as this, for in one day, suddenly a nation, Israel shall be born. More than 25 Bible predictions concerning Palestine have been fulfilled, many of them in the last century. More than 2,500 years ago Ezekiel spoke of God's judgments upon the enemies of Israel, and the Battle of Armageddon. Ezekiel's powerful prophecies strongly suggest that the Battle of Armageddon will be decided by nuclear warfare. Scriptures are very specific about how the land must be cleaned after the battle. Carefully bury the dead and burn the enemy weapons. These acts clearly point to radioactive contamination after nuclear warfare. The Bible is full of strange circumstances predicted thousands of years ago, that we are discovering today as scientific facts. To truly understand the Bible one must first understand the Bible is supernatural in origin and there is no other book in the world that contains its powers, and it is no ordinary book, but rather it is the *Living Word of God*. Explorer Christopher Columbus said the scriptures in the Bible inspired him to sail around the world to discover new worlds. Columbus spoke about a light in the heavens that led him to discover America. Did God guide Columbus to the New World America? Astonishing archaeological discoveries in the last century confirm the trustworthy provenance of many Bible scriptures and new evaluations very clearly outline amazing facts found that support the truth of our Bible.

REBIRTH OF ISRAEL

Jesus said to the world in Luke 21, *witness when Israel returns you will know I am God.*

2 Peter 3: 10 *"But the day of the Lord will come as a thief in the night, in which the Heaven will pass away with a great noise, and the elements will melt with fervent heat; both the earth and the world that are in it will be burned up."*

Chapter Ten

And then Ezekiel 39, written more than 2,500 years ago, tells us *God's judgment will fall upon the enemies of Israel.* Scripture speaks clearly of nuclear war.

11

Some Bible skeptics claim King David is only a biblical myth. Time magazine (circa 1993) confirmed that a stone tablet which had been found contained the inscription "House of David" and "King of Israel"; tests proved the writing was from the 9th Century BC, which was very close to King David's reign. This fantastic discovery is solid proof of the true existence of King David's life. So many archaeological finds lend credence to the authenticity of the Holy Bible. Nearly 50 years ago a stone tablet was uncovered near the ancient seat of Rome. The inscription on that tablet read "Pontius Pilate", and it gives me chills to think of the wonder of these things. Between the years of 1946-1956, Bedouin shepherds and a team of archaeologists made some more dramatic discoveries. The Dead Sea Scrolls were found hidden inside clay pots in a series of twelve or so clifftop caves, known as the "Ein Feshkha Caves" near the Dead Sea in the West Bank (then part of Jordan). After carbon testing, these scrolls proved to be great evidence for showing the truth of Bible scriptures for any skeptics and both confirmed and reaffirmed the reliability of the Old Testament. Carbon testing also provides provenance and supports important facts that these scrolls were written about the same time as Jesus' time on Earth. These scrolls give us a veritable treasure trove in the support of genuine biblical facts. Other archeological digs have unearthed human remains with iron nails still lodged in foot and heel bones. There is evidence that proves iron nails were used in the wrists and not in the hands of the crucified man's remains. Many of these nail-pierced bones are carbon dated to the time of Jesus. The uniqueness of Jesus' life is proven by Bible prophecies and scriptures which are in complete harmony with archeologies' amazing findings. The Bible came to us through the ages, an unfailing source of faith and spiritual strength, a book of wisdom and prophecies. God caused the Bible to be written to give divine inspiration and to guide his children through life, to comfort us in dark and frightening places and to become a beacon of hope and comfort. The Bible gives all the knowledge man needs to fill his longing soul and solve all his problems. Paul told us, *All scripture is given by inspiration of God.* Jesus' clear, bold message that every Christian with the hope of salvation must follow Him with their hearts. [And to love God with all their hearts, and with all their souls, and with all their minds and above all, have no other Gods but Him, the first law of The Ten Commandments]. Jesus taught quietly and tenderly how we should love one another. Something I hope I will help you realize sooner in your lives, and because I didn't realize it sooner myself, is that Bible reading is essential and should become a part of our daily lives. Thousands of questions about God are revealed in this holy book we call the Bible. Sometimes we struggle with trying to understand God; Who is he? What is he? And where is he? How can there be such a supreme being? Read your Bibles, prayerfully read your Bibles, asking God for understanding and His Word will be revealed to you. When you read the four gospels of Matthew, Mark, Luke and John, you will become aware of these great men of widely different personalities and writing styles. You will see the powerful, universal truth that underlies all gospel teachings. It will become abundantly clear what Paul meant

Chapter Eleven

when he said, *"Jesus Christ the same yesterday, and today, and forever"*. Knowledge of the Bible is essential for our daily lives, its pages are full of rich, meaningful inspiration and sound advice, it can counsel us and guide us. The Bible tells us that Jesus knows no limitations, He can be everywhere at once, He can see all, hear all, and know all. His power is immense and immeasurable. The beauty of God is indescribable. He is still performing miracles today throughout the world. His power, wisdom and love are limitless. He can change the course of the world at any moment, He can remove kings and replace leaders as fast as the blink of an eye. God can control all the wonders of our world and make changes at any time. Some people today in our modern style churches doubt that the Bible is the true word of God, they become doubters and unwilling to ascribe to God anything they cannot achieve themselves, feeling that all miracles and wonders ceased and desisted once Jesus ascended to be with his Father in Heaven. Jesus is still with us and He is right now performing mighty miracles on Earth; I know this because I have witnessed the might and beauty and power of God. God knows no limits. Some openly say they doubt the Bible as the true Word of God and just as openly like twisting the scriptures to fit their sinful lifestyles. Reiterating here, it is difficult for some to accept the unlimited power of God. Bible scriptures tell us God is our *light* when it seems the darkest, declaring Him the supreme one without flaw or blemish or faults and weaknesses. When Jesus spoke about his father, he said, "God is spirit". Jesus had a great vision of his father and is utterly perfect in describing every detail, so full of majestic righteousness. Jesus understood men's souls would be lost forever if his father had not sent him to die for sin; that his ultimate death by crucifixion was his purpose and his mission in order to save us from our sinful selves. Our founding fathers recognized the importance of building our nation on faith. These brave, patriotic men understood the truth of God and the true authority of the Bible. Realizing a Republic without morals could not subsist any length of time, these courageous men wrote our constitution based on the teachings of Jesus Christ. **Our nation's best security will be based on our love for Jesus Christ.** We are a united nation and our rights come from God. Our humble forefathers knew this and realized a republic built on religion and sound morals were the only foundation for public liberty and happiness. Following is a few words spoken from courageous leaders who pledged their lives for God and Nation:

President George Washington - "It is impossible to rightly govern the world without the word of God. It is the duty of every nation to acknowledge and obey Almighty God's every word."

President John Adams - "The Bible is the best book the world has ever seen. It contains more knowledge than all our libraries the world over, it should be the only law book for all. It teaches us how to love with kindness and charity toward others."

President Thomas Jefferson - "The Bible will teach us to become better husbands, fathers and citizens."

President James Madison - " The future of American civilization depends on the capacity of mankind for self-government, we must sustain ourselves according to the Ten Commandments."

President John Quincy Adams - "There is no other

Chapter Eleven

book like the Bible, it must be read every day by all ages. It is a necessity to our everyday life."

President Andrew Jackson - "The Bible is the rock on which our republic rests."

President Abraham Lincoln - "I believe God's greatest gift to the world is the Bible that gives us peace and strength." And Mr. Lincoln further stated, "America will never be destroyed from the outside, if we falter and lose our freedom, it will be because we destroyed ourselves."

President Woodrow Wilson - "I faithfully believe solutions to all man's problems can be found when you faithfully study God's words."

President Herbert Hoover - "The Bible is the inspiration of our civilization and fundamentals of American life."

President Franklin D. Roosevelt - "It is a fountain of strength and the highest aspirations of the human soul. The Bible is important for our nation's development. "

President Dwight D. Eisenhower - "The Bible is a book of inspiration for wisdom. Anyone that denies the existence and supernatural powers of God is a stupid fool." [Amen.]

President Ronald Reagan - Reagan believed the answers to all mankind's problems could be answered within the covers of the Bible, he said, "the Bible can touch hearts and refresh souls."

Patriot John Hancock - "We recognize no sovereign but God, and no king but Jesus."

Part Two

Great Leaders

Oral Roberts

Pentecostal preacher Oral Roberts burst on the scene as one of the very first pioneers of televised ministry, with his healing/revival program which gave religion a new voice and created an exciting new era for Christians in America. This charismatic, Pentecostal preacher inspired millions and in 1954 his crusades were televised all over the nation. In time, there would come many other televangelists following in his footsteps. Roberts's life and ministry would draw much attention and not a little controversy, calling into question both his fundraising tactics and luxurious lifestyle.

When Roberts was young the devil tried to take his life and silence his voice, but he fought back, going on to preach as he understood the old adage, the Lord works in mysterious ways [paraphrased]. Oral Roberts truly was a great man of God. Pastor Roberts often recalled times when their poor family had barely enough food to feed the five Roberts kids, being two boys and three girls. His father was a revival minister who scratched out enough money for his family and himself to just survive.

When Oral was in school, he was silent because he suffered a terrible problem with stuttering so that every time he said anything he was laughed at and bullied. The bullying became so bad that at age 16 he moved away from his family to another town seeking peace in his troubled life. A year later, at 17 Oral collapsed while playing basketball and so returned to his family where he lay bedridden for five months, having suffered yet another collapse. He lost weight and coughed up blood and was examined by several doctors who agreed the news was indeed bad, that Oral had contracted Tuberculosis in both lungs. It was looking rather hopeless for Oral with the diagnosis of this killer disease as most people diagnosed with Tuberculosis didn't get better and recover from it. The family often prayed long and hard at Oral's bedside. Oral was extremely close to his mom and one day asked her why God gave him this bad disease. His mother told him, God loves you, he didn't make you sick, it is the work of the devil trying to destroy you so you can't do God's work, he also is the cause of your stuttering problem. Then Oral's mother told him about when she was pregnant with him, explaining to him how God had spoken to her while he was in her womb, telling her that she would have a son and that he would preach the Gospel and become a great healer. His mom further explained to him the devil made him sick in an effort to stop Oral from doing God's work, trying to silence Oral from preaching God's Gospel. The entire Roberts family continuously prayed at Oral's bedside. One day as Oral's father prayed Oral saw the face of Jesus so perfectly clear that he jumped from his bed shouting how God had healed him from the terrible disease. He also heard God's voice telling him, "you shall be healed". He said that on that day he felt the Holy Spirit of God enter into him. It was almost impossible for anyone who knew young Oral to believe the sickly, frail, stuttering boy would ever amount to anything, whether he lived or not. Because of the family's prayers and unwavering belief in the supernatural power of God's healing, the young Oral's health improved greatly over the ensuing months and he became stronger and eventually the stutter that had silenced him would slowly leave him. His doctors were shocked when they reexamined him realizing not only was he still alive but that he was totally healed of the dread Tuberculin.

Oral Roberts fought the good fight and defeated the devil that tried so hard to silence his voice and destroy his young body. After which, the newly healed Oral was ready to fulfill his mom's prophecy and go out into the world to preach and to heal others. Just a few months later the doctors indeed gave Oral a clean bill of health and so he started his small ministry, in fact after preaching his first sermon he acquired less than a dollar from the offering. However, he was not deterred, because he then decided to purchase a tent and ended up filling it to capacity and had to purchase an even larger tent as the crowds of followers continued flowing in. At one particular tent revival twenty-two thousand people came to hear the Gospel and to be healed. Roberts healed by the practice of laying on of hands and through the power of God he cast out demons. He stopped in the middle of one sermon and boldly asked that the three people in the crowd who were thinking about suicide to please come forward. The three came down front to him and he laid hands on them and saved their souls. Roberts's ministry reached millions as he held crusades on six continents, and consequently leading millions to Christ.

In 1954 he was one of the first persons to preach on television though many pastors would follow in his footsteps.

In 1963 he established the Oral Roberts University in Tulsa, Oklahoma, a private evangelical liberal arts institution accredited by the Higher Learning Commission.

In 1981 he opened the doors to Faith Medical and Research Center, also in Oklahoma.

He published a monthly magazine called "Healing Waters" and he wrote many books on healing power.

God healed Oral Roberts so that he could bring the Gospel of Christ to the masses. No one can deny this man was a true and loyal servant of God. Even though in his youth the odds were overwhelmingly stacked against him, through courage and faith which was coupled with a deep devotion to his God, he fought to live and to fulfill his purpose in life serving and healing others until his own death. Oral Roberts said that when you see a miracle, you see God - Don't let anyone tell you that miracles cannot happen in your life. God is inseparable from miracles. The Reverend Billy Graham had often spoken fondly of Oral, saying, "Oral Roberts was a man of God and a great friend in ministry. I loved him like a brother." But, Oral Roberts's adult life was not all one big bed of roses, he had his trials and family sorrows just as we all experience. And so it was that in 1982 Roberts's gay, drug addicted son committed suicide. Even as the family grieved, the media shamefully mocked Roberts's lack of parenting skills. But no media sensationalism can take away the fact that when Pentecostal preacher Oral Roberts burst on the scene as one of the very first pioneers of televised ministry, with his healing/revival program he gave religion a new voice and created an exciting new era for Christians in America. This charismatic, Pentecostal preacher inspired millions and in 1954 his crusades were televised all over the nation. In time, there would come many other televangelists because they were following his example. And it is true that Roberts's life and ministry would draw much attention and controversy, calling into question his fundraising tactics and luxurious lifestyle. But this cannot dim his light, because after all was said and done Oral Roberts accomplished many great and wonderful things in the name of the Lord. He was a man of great faith and did much for many.

William Franklin Graham, Jr.

On November 7, 1918, William Franklin Graham, Jr., known as "Billy" Graham was born on a dairy farm near Charlotte, North Carolina. Billy's parents were devout Presbyterians with Scots-Irish ancestry, and like many others of that harsh time period, Billy's father lost most of the family's savings in the 1929 stock market crash. They suffered but the dairy farm always provided enough food to eat and all the milk the family could consume. The dairy work was long, hard hours both day and night, and the Graham family was poor like many other folks from this time in our nation's history. Later in life Billy would tell how his parents taught their children that laziness is evil, but that there is dignity and honor in hard labor.

After high school in 1936, young Billy attended a small college in Tennessee for a short period of time, but his deeply religious parents urged him to transfer to a Bible-based college in Florida, the Florida Bible Institute. While attending this Florida college, the students were encouraged to go out into the local community and preach to anyone willing to listen. Billy spent many hours practicing his preaching skills to local churches, both on the streets and sidewalks and even outside the bars in some places.

After graduation in 1940 Billy moved to Illinois and continued his spiritual training and education at Wheaton College about 25 miles west of Chicago, where he met and fell in love with Ruth Bell, a fellow student whose parents were Presbyterian missionaries, her father, Nelson being a missionary-surgeon. Billy and

Ruth were married on August 13, 1943 and the newlyweds settled near Wheaton where Billy became Pastor of the First Baptist Church in Western Springs, Illinois. Billy's confidence grew with each sermon he delivered, preaching love, forgiveness and the need to repent. Shortly after becoming the pastor of this first church, he met a man named Torrey Johnson. Johnson approached Billy and offered to turn over his Sunday night radio ministry to him. So Billy went before his church board and with their approval was told to give it a try. Not long after Billy went on the air, listeners' mail began to pour in for the show, thus the Reverend Billy Graham had just taken his first steps toward fame. With every subsequent show, Graham sharpened his skills, feeling and becoming very natural and confident, knowing he was doing what God intended for his life. Radio listeners invited him to speak at various events and gatherings. Then in 1947, Dr. W. B. Riley, President of Northwestern Bible College asked Graham to speak at his college. Reverend Riley was in failing health and after Billy Graham fulfilled his speaking commitment there, the ailing minister asked Billy Graham to become his successor as President of Northwestern Schools, a group of Christian schools in Minnesota. The young Billy humbly protested at first but finally agreed to serve in this capacity until a permanent leader became available. Just months later, the Reverend Riley passed away and Billy Graham remained there until 1952, when he resigned to concentrate all his efforts on preaching. During his time at Northwestern, back in 1949 Graham was invited to hold a series of revival meetings in Los Angeles, California. The young Graham labeled Los Angeles a "wicked city full of sin", the irony is not lost here with the translation being *The Angels*. The revival was held in a Ringling Brothers' circus tent and drew modest crowds in the beginning. After the revival newspaper mogul William Randolph Hearst's newspapers around the country gave Graham's revival great press reviews. It felt like overnight that Graham became a media sensation, stories ran in Life magazine, Time magazine and Newsweek magazine highlighting Graham's Los Angeles revival. The Press told Billy Graham, "you have been kissed by William Randolph Hearst". Suddenly the tent meetings overflowed to hear the young preacher who was so charismatic delivering his heartfelt gospel messages. Hollywood celebrities John Wayne, Roy Rogers, Gene Autrey and film producer Cecil B. DeMille flocked to the tent, along with famous athletes and many other prominent and plain citizens of Los Angeles; they all came out to see and hear this new "star", this religious star. Now, given all this Billy Graham never even met Hearst and he never knew exactly why the media tycoon promoted him so much, a fact I find interesting. (My wife says it was a God-thing, or a God-wink) But, soon after the Los Angeles revival breakthrough Graham followed up with revivals in Boston, Massachusetts and Columbia, South Carolina. Graham was fast becoming a household name across the nation. And less than a year after his first revivals he put together a team of trusted friends who organized The Billy Graham Evangelistic Association, and thereby launched a weekly radio program called "The Hour of Decision" as well as a national newspaper column printed in 99 newspapers all across America. The weekly radio program was broadcast on almost a thousand different stations. Even the Pope said Graham was the most popular, talked-about Christian leader in the world. Graham took his crusades overseas to Korea, France, Holland and Germany; people flocked to hear him speak and he filled sports stadiums, tents and open-air arenas with folks hungering for the Word. Reverend Graham used every technique possible to get his message of Christ to the masses. Graham would tell people that he used these various techniques because, "I'm selling the greatest product in the world!" Indeed, although he was humble about his fame, he was anything but humble about giving God the glory, saying he was only a "tool of God" - his strong sermons were always simple and pure as he attacked sin and saved multitudes of souls.

Graham was fascinated with our presidents and he first met Harry Truman at the White House in 1950. Later, Graham would urge Truman to declare a National Day of Prayer and a Proclamation came to fruition on April 17, 1952: When Dwight D. Eisenhower became the nation's 34th President, he felt it important that faith should be the center of national life and so he was baptized in a private ceremony into the Presbyterian faith. A young Billy Graham presented the president with a beautiful Bible which he would keep by his bedside thereafter. In fact, Eisenhower initiated the National Prayer Breakfast and welcomed Reverend Billy Graham into the White House as a spiritual adviser and the two became good friends.

In 1955 The Gallup Poll named Billy Graham one of the ten most admired men in the world; over the years he would be honored 46 more times for this particular distinction. (In 1983 he received the Presidential Medal of Freedom {by President Ronald Reagan} and in 1996 he and his beloved wife, Ruth were the recipients of the Congressional Gold Medal). In the sixties, Billy also took a liking to the young President John Kennedy and on occasion enjoyed playing a round of golf or two with the young leader. Billy Graham also visited often with close friend Lyndon Johnson, both at the White House and at Johnson's Texas ranch as the two " farm boys" shared a close relationship. Graham stood strong with his support of Johnson's Civil Rights Act of 1964, marching beside Dr. Martin Luther King, Jr. and doing everything he possibly could to help break down any racial barriers. Later on Graham often visited President Nixon at the White House and at first had a very favorable opinion of that President. This was all before the fiasco ensued during the Watergate years. After the Watergate incident was a very painful time for Graham, and years later he said that Nixon disappointed him, that he had misjudged him and felt as if Nixon had used their friendship for self-gain, and admittedly, he had been naive about his friendship with and about the man Nixon. But Graham also had many warm visits in the White House, such as visiting with Ronald and Nancy Reagan. On March 30, 1981 Nancy asked their friend Billy Graham to come to the hospital to pray with her at Ronald's bedside after he was shot in an assassination attempt and Billy did so. Now Graham liked both President Bushes and had a warm and enduring friendship with the entire Bush family. Regarding President Bill Clinton he had different views of the man, but was impressed with his strong charisma. Graham had first met Clinton when Bill was the Governor of Arkansas. At that time he was so impressed with the highly intelligent Clinton that he told others, "that young man is so full of charisma he would make a great evangelist if he chose to preach".

Graham himself never had any political aspirations or ambitions, but he remained fascinated by the various Presidents' courage in difficult times, understanding the heavy burdens these great leaders dealt with every day and he watched each one as they both prematurely and quickly aged with the weight of the world on their shoulders. At times he prayed with these great leaders and provided them divine strength and encouragement. At the time of Kennedy's assassination, (and as soon as the news reached Graham) he wired Lyndon Johnson and told him he was praying for him and his presidency. The Reverend Billy Graham was a great source of strength and encouragement for our leaders when they were in their hour of need and when they most needed some God-motivated power. One of my favorite quotes from Reverend Graham is when he said, "Someday you will read or hear that Billy Graham is dead. Don't you believe a word of it. I shall be more alive than I am now. I have just changed my address!" The moment we take our last breath on Earth we take our first in Heaven.

As I write about Graham's life I can close my eyes and still envision this great minister and man of God behind a pulpit in an open-air stadium holding an open Bible in his right hand even as his left arm was outstretched, a long finger pointing at a massive crowd inviting people to come forward to receive Christ. And I can almost "hear" those wonderful old hymns from the crusades, being led by George Beverly Shea as if he were present right now singing the invitational. And literally hundreds of people would respond, hundreds came forward to accept Jesus Christ as their personal Savior. How marvelous it is that Billy Graham helped thousands upon thousands of souls enter into the kingdom of Heaven! Every time I think of the little boy who gave his two small fish (from the Gospel of John) and five loaves of bread to feed thousands who came to hear Jesus preach I am humbled because that little boy could have held back and only given a portion of his food, but for Christ he gave everything he had. He did not hold anything back from Jesus, he simply trusted. Billy Graham was like that little boy, in that every time he preached he kept the sermons simple and pure and his words traveled straight down into people's collective souls, telling the masses that God loves you, God forgives your sins, come down and receive the Lord. Graham gave his all for Christ and never held back.

The Bible tells us that John the Baptist preached loudly from the banks of the Jordan River about the first coming of Jesus Christ. Well, Billy Graham preached to billions about the second coming of Jesus Christ. Graham said, "I was certain I was right with God." There is no doubt in my mind if Billy Graham had been standing near John the Baptist on the banks of the Jordan River at the time Jesus walked up that he would have chosen Billy to be one of his disciples. For six decades he blessed the world with his message of Christ. Now he is blessing Heaven with his presence. As of February 21, 2018 Heaven has just become a more beautiful place with Billy Graham there. It is absolutely amazing to me how God took an ordinary, lanky-framed, young boy from a North Carolina dairy farm and turned him into the greatest evangelist of the 20th Century. The young fire and brimstone preacher with his distinctive Carolinian drawl was no ordinary man. The young, once upon a time door-to-door salesman was without a doubt anointed by God to do His work, preaching in the beginning to small churches and in tents, and later preaching in bigger tents, huge stadiums and large sports arenas being televised worldwide. Billy was a true blessing and a gift from God to the people of this planet. It is my firm belief that Billy Graham was anointed by God. Let it be known that Billy Graham once said, "I was certain I was right with God."

Martin Luther King, Jr.

On January 15, 1929 Martin Luther King, Jr. was born into a family of preachers. His father, grandfather, brother, and an uncle were all pastors of Baptist churches. Martin said planning his future was no hard choice, that he would carry on with family tradition and preach. At a young age Martin witnessed the brutal ugliness of racism. Once a white woman slapped his face in a store claiming he stepped on her foot. Another time a white bus rider made him get up out of his seat so he could then sit down. Martin stood for more than an hour in the aisle of that bus as the white man enjoyed the comfort of his seat. The man seated there on that day had no idea and indeed no way of knowing that that young boy standing in the aisle near him would one day become one of the most important men of the 20th century. Martin was born in Atlanta, Georgia and attended the all black Booker T. Washington High School where he excelled in his classes. He possessed a strong, dynamic personality yet was very gentle and maintained a deeply religious attitude. Martin witnessed firsthand the many brutalities of the deep south. The hatred meted out by the Ku Klux Klan and the beatings and hangings of innocent people. Even so, Martin never strayed from his Christian doctrine of loving his enemies, even those who were saturated with hatred.

In September of 1944 Martin started his freshman year at Morehouse College where he would receive his Bachelor's Degree in Sociology. At Morehouse College the professors encouraged their students to discuss racial problems. Martin found a new calling to make a difference, knowing in his heart of hearts that the black movement was right and the time was right to act on this calling, purporting that if we be wrong then so will God Almighty be wrong. Martin's calling was urging him to serve society by breaking down the barriers of hate, and he looked to his father who at one time served as President of the Atlanta NAACP and worked hard for moral justice. Young Martin was starting to show an interest in breaking down the unfair social barriers and at 19 years of age entered Crozer Theological Seminary in Chester, Pennsylvania attending from 1948 through 1951 and receiving a Bachelor's Degree from that facility. One day he attended a lecture on the life and teachings of Mahatma Gandhi and that lecture had a deep impact on his thinking, therefore he became fascinated with Gandhi and the notion of nonviolent resistance concerning social reform. Gandhi's message was a philosophy to love your enemies, and to exercise the power of love even for those who may hate you. Young Martin readily adopted Gandhi's philosophy of love and nonviolence, and he felt the power of love to be a potent instrument which could change and reform society for the betterment of all people everywhere. Martin always had an optimistic view regarding human nature and believed in the goodness of mankind. Regardless of the dark tragedies of history, he believed that one day all mankind could live together in a moral society. He chose to confront evil by the power of love.

Then one day a close friend introduced Martin to a young, attractive Coretta Scott who had aspirations of being a concert singer and he soon realized Coretta was everything he ever wanted in a woman and that she shared his strong faith in God and his strong quest for racial justice. So it was that on June 18, 1953 Martin's father performed the wedding ceremony for the young couple. The newly wedded Kings decided to make their first home in Boston for a time. Several churches there expressed an interest in young Martin serving as their pastor. But it was the historic Dexter Avenue Baptist Church in Montgomery, Alabama that enticed the Kings to move from Boston. Dexter Baptist Church had invited young King to deliver a trial sermon on the 24th of January, 1954 and several months later Martin accepted the call to serve as their new minister. He was installed in this new capacity on October 31st of 1954, nine months after offering that demo sermon. Every Sunday morning Martin got up early so he could spend quiet time meditating and praying before delivering his sermons from the pulpit of the historic church. The congregation was very receptive and impressed with their new pastor, the young Martin. As full time minister Martin tended to the needs of his congregation by visiting the sick and helping anyone in need. It was a very happy time for all of them and he felt comfortable with this new life. Even though Martin and Coretta understood the northern part of the country offered them more opportunity and privileges with less discrimination and more advantages to grow, they both felt a moral obligation to return to the problems that plagued the deep south. And where better to perform his type of ministry than to live in the heart of the matter! King felt he could better serve God and mankind from there and would stand up against racial discrimination, playing a crucial role in helping the oppressed.

On December 1, 1955 a middle-aged seamstress named Rosa Parks refused to give up her bus seat to a rude, white passenger. The bus operator demanded she get up and relinquish her bus seat to the pompous white man. Ms. Parks, who happened to be black, refused to move, stating emphatically she would no longer accept this type of disrespect. Almost immediately she was arrested, bodily removed from the bus and taken to jail where she was fingerprinted and fined $14.00 plus court costs, no small sum in those days. Because of her courageous act of refusing to sacrifice her dignity any longer she sparked the Civil Rights Movement. Martin Luther King, Jr., and the Reverend Ralph Abernathy, along with other black civic leaders called for a bus boycott. On Sunday all of Montgomery's black ministers told their memberships not to ride the buses anymore, but to find alternate means of transportation and that people could share rides or carpool to make it possible to stay off the buses. Seventy percent of the bus riders in Montgomery were black and so after just a few days of buses running with mostly empty seats, this made a tremendous impact on the bus line's revenues. Three hundred and eighty-two days later the boycott was over and history was made. The United States Supreme Court voted Montgomery's segregated seating unconstitutional and when this boycott was ended Reverend King, Jr. was the first passenger giving his approval. Rosa Parks' refusal to move from her bus seat triggered the spark the nation needed to ignite the Civil Rights Movement and Ms. Parks became known as The Mother Of The Civil Rights Movement. This grand lady would spend the rest of her life working inside the NAACP fighting injustices. In 1996 Ms. Parks was awarded the Medal Of Freedom and in 1999 received the Congressional Gold Medal. Indeed, the bus boycott was the beginning of a long struggle for the civil rights of millions of American blacks. For the next thirteen years King urged people to protest unjust treatment, and to do this out of a spirit of love, encouraging people to work hard to break the chains of hatred and evil. King told audiences that one day he may be found dead, admonishing them not to react with violence or to retaliate. King said the voice of Jesus told him to fight on the principle that "a change is coming". From Montgomery,

Alabama to Washington, DC King lead marches, the participants with their arms and hands linked together signifying unity sang the battle hymn of the civil rights movement, "We Shall Overcome". Often these brave marchers were treated with brutal, hate-filled ugliness, sustaining beatings, dog bites and even having fire hoses turned on them. King would be arrested more than 20 times on fake charges made by hate-filled policemen. King's home was bombed, as well as several churches. On September 15, 1963 a dynamite bomb killed four young black girls while they were having Bible class at a Birmingham Baptist church. The innocent little girls' deaths were some of the most vicious and heinous crimes against the Civil Rights Movement. King delivered the eulogy at three of these girls' funerals. Just a few days after the girls' funerals, President John F. Kennedy met with Reverend King and other black leaders and the Civil Rights Movement found a strong ally in President Kennedy, who worked closely with King to pass legislation to support the movement. Because Kennedy had grown up in the northeast it was at first hard for him to grasp the cruel treatment of blacks in the south. But once he realized the hardships and unfairness to blacks he made a personal promise to make changes and exercised every opportunity to advance the Civil Rights Movement along with his younger brother, Robert. Both Kennedys understood segregation was morally wrong, and with the Kennedy's support the racial barriers were beginning to come down and freedom was in sight. Around this time period, King said that Richard Nixon was the most dangerous man in America. In a letter penned by King he stated Nixon had a way of convincing others of his sincerity for their cause, but that he [Nixon] was a fake and an opportunist. It seems King was indeed a great judge of character.

In August of 1963 at the Washington, DC Lincoln Memorial, he addressed a crowd of 250,000 listeners and told them, "I Have A Dream". This became a landmark speech as indeed Dr. King had a dream, and his words and his mission resonate still today. As a child of the fifties, I can even now fairly hear the sound of his voice as it emitted from our television set (l know, but this is what we called tvs in the "olden days").

Five years later, on April 3rd, 1968 in Memphis, Tennessee the Reverend King addressed a crowd and told them about the difficult days ahead, also telling them he had been to the mountaintop and he didn't mind that he was only permitted to look; but like anybody, he would like to live a long life, longevity has its place after all, but that he was not overly concerned with this at that particular time because he just wanted to do God's will. Saying that God had allowed him to go up to the mountain, look over, and see the Promised Land. Continuing, he said that he may not get there with us but he wanted us to know that night, that we the people, we will get into the Promised Land, saying he was happy that night, and that he was not worried or anxious about anything. That he feared no man, because his eyes had seen the coming of the Lord. To our nation's shock and sadness, less than 24 hours after telling that certain Memphis audience that God had allowed him to go up to that mountain-top and view the Promised Land but that he himself might not get there WITH them, he was assassinated. Did King have a strong premonition his time had finally run out? Perhaps so, as King often spoke of hearing God's own voice telling him to "fight on". Did King have a special connection with God, was he like the apostle Paul, an extremist who fought for the Gentiles and their right to worship God? I truly believe both men were anointed by the hand of God to change the world in troubled times for the betterment of all mankind. King had adopted Gandhi's ways of nonviolence and lived his life sincerely dedicated to this premise. From 1957 until his ironically violent death in 1968, King had traveled more than six million miles and had made more than twenty-five hundred speeches regarding the importance for all of mankind to live in love and peace. He captured the attention of the entire world.

To my way of thinking, The Reverend Doctor Martin Luther King, Jr., was our 20th Century Moses, leading millions to the Promised Land. And like Moses, he did not enter with his people.

Just a few notable accomplishments and a bit of trivia about Rev. Dr. King:

* He was born Michael Luther King, Jr.
* He wrote five books
* He was awarded five honorary degrees
* He was chosen as Time Magazine's Man of the Year 1963
* At age thirty-five he became the youngest man to receive the Nobel Peace Prize
* He was a symbolic leader for Civil Rights, (actually having been elected the President of the Southern Christian Leadership Conference in 1957)

On the evening of April 4, 1968 King was assassinated while standing on a balcony outside his hotel room in Memphis, Tennessee. Our Moses of the 20th Century was gone but he shall never be forgotten.

False Leaders

Jim Jones

Some of you may remember Jim Jones, a strong minded young minister who started his ministry in Indianapolis, Indiana. His church served free meals to the needy and preached the Gospel and fought hard for other's civil rights. In 1963 Jones moved his ministry to San Francisco, California where he had several thousand loyal followers. As time passed, the Reverend Jones began showing signs of extremism and fanaticism, which would manifest into extreme anger and paranoia and he would swallow large amounts of pills which in turn fueled his anger and paranoia. At times he made irrational claims that he was the reincarnation of Jesus Christ. The more mentally unstable he became, Jones' inflated ego, along with his increasingly heavy use of drugs, would spin his life completely and tragically out of control. The problem with this scenario is that he took many of his followers with him on this downward spiral. Jones decided to move his People's Temple ministry to the jungle of Guyana to flee U.S. religious persecution. Not long after the move to Guyana, a California congressman, Leo Ryan was approached by concerned relatives of temple members. These relatives told Congressman Ryan they were fearful for the welfare of their loved ones and asked the congressman to investigate and hopefully ease their anxieties. Ryan contacted the U.S. Embassy in Georgetown and asked if they could go out to the colony and check on the welfare of the members. The report came back to Ryan, telling him everyone was fine and that not one member spoke any desire to leave the colony. But the troubling rumors kept coming in to the congressman concerning the conduct of the Reverend Jim Jones and his increasingly violent outbursts of temper and erratic behaviors. Those continuing claims prompted Congressman Ryan to go to the jungle himself and have a look around to determine if there were indeed problems that needed to be addressed. He arrived in Guyana with an entourage of more than a dozen people, some were news correspondents and photographers while others were close relatives of temple members hoping they could speak with and persuade their kin to return home with them, leaving the remote jungle colony behind. As soon as Ryan and his delegation arrived they were warmly greeted and given a tour of the colony. They were impressed with the nice school which had a large library, and there was even a hospital with a nursery so that colony babies could be born with proper care in case of birthing problems. They inspected the newly built sawmill along with a large open air pavilion provided for assembling to preach and to play. On this particular day a colony band provided entertainment for the visitors, playing a variety of happy tunes under the large pavilion's canopy for the curious guests. Congressman Ryan was very impressed and starting to feel good about the jungle colony when suddenly a chain of events unfolded that completely changed the course of the visit. One of the temple members slipped a note to newsman Don Harris of NBC News. Contained in the note was information that the note bearer and several others actually wanted to leave, to return to their U.S. homes and families. The visitors then asked the Reverend Jones how he would feel if some of his members wanted to leave with them, to which Jones replied members could come and go as they pleased. Then newsman Harris asked Jones about rumors of large stockpiles of guns on the property and heavily armed guards, at which point Jones just came unglued and cried out it was all lies. Jones behavior became very disturbing, provoking the congressman to quickly gather his group and the few members wanting to leave and head for the airstrip. At the airstrip, as the group was waiting outside the plane before takeoff, suddenly all the members of the colony's guard arrived and began shooting everyone near the planes. The assailants killed Ryan, Brown, newsman Harris and Examiner photographer Greg Robinson, who all lay dead on the jungle airstrip as one small Cessna aircraft managed to take off with five surviving passengers. Ten others who were wounded managed to escape into the safety of the jungle. The gunmen then returned to the colony and reported to Jones about the killings at the airstrip. Jones called all his followers to the pavilion as nurses carried containers full of a poisoned fruit drink to the crowd where Jones instructed everyone to line up and drink. Some drank willingly while others were forced at gunpoint to drink the juice laced with Cyanide. Jones warned the crowd that if any should survive they would be hunted down by the Guyanese Army and be castrated and tortured without mercy. Jones' own body was found lying beside his large chair with a bullet wound to his head. When the chaos quelled, hundreds lay dead. The final count of dead bodies numbered 918. A tape recording was found at the site of the mass suicide with Jones' voice clearly encouraging followers to kill themselves, admonishing them, *"Let's get on with this, for God's sake"*. It took only one day for Jim Jones to turn the Peoples' Temple into the Temple of Doom.

Marshall Herff Applewhite

On March 22, 1997 thirty-eight devoted followers of Marshall Herff Applewhite, of the Heaven's Gate religious cult were found dead along with their leader from suicide inside a beautiful Rancho Santa Fe mansion. (Rancho Santa Fe is an exclusive suburb of San Diego, California.) What brought about this gruesome discovery is that a former cult member received a Federal Express package containing two video tapes showing cult members happily talking about taking their own lives and looking forward to their new kingdom where they would be joining up with their new alien families. The very worried former cult member drove to the Santa Fe mansion where he opened the front door and was assailed by the putrid stench of death. He immediately notified the San Diego Sheriffs office. Upon arriving at the scene the officers could scarce believe what they found inside that house of death. All cult members had taken a cocktail of drugs and vodka mixed with pudding. They then placed tightly sealed plastic bags over their heads and awaited their transportation to the new realm. All of these people were found on bunk beds, dressed in black clothes which included new black colored Nike sneakers. There were twenty-one women and eighteen men; six of the men including Applewhite, had been castrated. The group killed themselves so they could catch a ride on a supposed spaceship that was to arrive at the time of the Hale-Bopp comet, and this spaceship would then deliver them to their new planet home in the universe. Applewhite, a former choir teacher from Texas had once been arrested for credit card fraud and car theft, but he claimed to be a representative for the aliens that would be arriving with the comet in a spaceship and that they all would receive new bodies and souls and then would be transported into the universe to a new planet home. It is hard to comprehend how a former choir teacher and car thief could have convinced 38 people to kill themselves. Even the best cult experts have had trouble trying to understand this group. Family members were allowed to watch their loved ones on the video tapes talking about ending their earthly lives so they could go live on another planet with new alien friends. One woman cult member said on that tape that people would think she had completely "lost all her marbles" but they would be wrong, because she had made a great choice. Surviving families just wanted to make sense out of this tragic event as they tried desperately to find some kind of closure, but this proved to be a nearly impossible feat as this tragedy defied any event experienced heretofore by others anywhere in the world. Applewhite was the son of a Presbyterian minister with a promising career as a music professor, he was married with two children and often sang with the Houston Grand Opera in his native Texas. Nothing in his formative years, nothing in his previous lifestyle gave any indication of what was to become of his life. Applewhite gave up everything for Heaven's Gate. And the people who died along with Applewhite were very ordinary members of society, these people were made up of a nurse, an outdoorsman, a computer expert, and a homemaker and mother of five children, just to state a point of reference. How I wish these good people could have found God instead of Marshall Herff Applewhite.

David Koresh

On February 28, 1993 federal agents arrived at the Branch Davidians' compound just outside Waco, Texas to serve two warrants there; one for child abuse and the other for illegal weapons. The raid quickly escalated into a vicious battle resulting in the deaths of four lawmen and five cult members. The number of dead could have been much higher if not for the cult members cease fire that allowed FBI and ATF agents a chance to retreat with their wounded and dead to a safe distance enabling them to receive emergency medical help. The deadly gun battle led to a difficult 51 day siege that kept our nation on edge as people watched daily news coverage of the horrific events that unfolded at the Branch Davidian compound. Midway through the siege, leader David Koresh allowed 37 of his followers to leave the compound; this was fortunate for the 21 children and 16 adults allowed this privilege, because after their release, negotiations seemed to stall. As negotiators listened to Koresh's irrational claims of "I am your God and you will bow under my feet. Do you think you have the power to stop my will? ", he rambled on for days claiming to open the seven seals and foresee the end of the world. All federal negotiations efforts seemed hopeless at this point. Tragically, the man claiming to be God and still holding a number of women and children with him, refused to come out and end the long siege. After about six weeks, on April 18, 1993 newly appointed Attorney General Janet Reno called President Bill Clinton and briefed him on her plan to use tear gas on the compound to force the cult members to leave the building and thereby end the siege. So the next day, on April 19, 1993, the plan to end the siege began, but as soon as the gas was released into a corner of the compound, the women and children fled to the center of the second floor, and this action turned out to be a deadly decision. There they hunkered down, and with no exit door they became trapped in a blazing inferno. It is still a matter of question as to whether the military grade incendiary devices shot into the compound caused the ensuing fire; or whether David Koresh himself set the fire that soon engulfed the building, and which raged quickly out of control. The fire, fueled by 30 plus mph winds on that fateful day, sent flames racing through the wooden structure, which caused stockpiles of ammunition to cook-off and explode inside the inferno. As onlookers gazed helplessly, they heard several loud explosions, which continued as the spreading flames were fed by the high prairie winds. The compound became fully engulfed with no hope of escape for most of those inside. The apocalyptic event which the young so-called messiah, David Koresh preached for so long had finally come to consume him and some members of his misled flock. Initially, four ATF agents and six Branch Davidians were killed in the beginning of the raid. Then the 51-day siege ensued, ending with the FBI assault in which the compound burned down, killing 76 people inside including David Koresh. Two dozen of the dead were children. Attorney Janet Reno faced sharp criticism for her handling of this terrible tragedy, as then President Bill Clinton, being his usual "slick" self, kept a safe distance from any blame. Sadly, this story doesn't end in the ashes of the Waco compound. On the second anniversary of the Waco siege, a man named Timothy McVeigh, with help from his friend, Terry Nichols parked a large truck filled with explosives in front of a federal building in Oklahoma City, Oklahoma. After

False Leaders

they detonated the explosives inside the truck, 150 innocent people died tragically, including 19 children attending a day care center inside that doomed building. Such needless, senseless human suffering.

Part Three

English Poet John Newton
1725-1807

John grew up with no religion to guide his life path. After serving in the Royal Navy he became involved in the slave trade. In 1748 off the coast of Ireland, a violent storm so severely battered his slave ship that he cried out to God in desperation, begging for God's Grace to save him and his ship. After this episode (although it took him a few years) he ended his slave trading career and parted ways with the sea, he found God and became a Christian and Clergyman. Shortly before the first day of 1773 John was preparing his New Year's Day sermon and as he put words on paper there is no doubt he was looking back at his past life of sin and feeling the powerful love of God and God's grace and forgiveness as he wrote the beautiful and inspired by God words to Amazing Grace. This beautiful and enduring hymn is easily the most famous folk hymn ever written. John gave the world an amazing gift with this song. As for myself, I cannot think of a more darkly violent sin than the slave trade. To take a person away from their home and family, their land and everything that is familiar and comfortable to their way of life and placing them in shackles in the bottom of a dank and dirty ship is such a horrendous travesty of humankind. Many of these poor souls perished in the bellies of these nasty ships, because of the violent passage and lack of any sanitation nor enough food to sustain life. I fear these perished souls may have been the more fortunate ones, because those who survived the journey were then sold like farm animals to the highest bidder into a life of confusion, despair and misery. Amazing Grace is my favorite song about forgiveness and redemption. It tells us that regardless of our sins, our souls can be delivered through God's unchallenged mercy and grace.

"I am not what I ought to be. I am not what I want to be. I am not what I hope to be. And by the grace of God I am what I am."

What a concept, a slave trader who found God and turned his life around and fought against slavery ... now this, my friends, is Amazing Grace.

Poet William Cowper

In 1773 the English poet William Cowper became so upset with life he decided to throw himself into the Thames River on a densely foggy Olney night. He found a cab and urged the driver to seek the embankment, but after being hopelessly lost in the thick fog for a considerable time he became impatient, and leapt out of the cab only to find himself standing smack in front of his own home once again. It is reported that he gave up the idea of suicide, went to his room and wrote the poem, Light Shining out of Darkness, the poem likely being the source of the now familiar phrase God moves in mysterious ways, although the first line of that poem actually reads "God moves in a mysterious way His wonders to perform; He plants His footsteps in the sea And rides upon the storm." That poem, being the last text for a hymn that Cowper wrote, was the one written following his attempted suicide that night. (John Newton actually published the poem the next year in his Twenty-six Letters on Religious Subjects; to which are added Hymns (1774).

Pastor Thomas Dorsey

When Pastor Thomas Dorsey wrote the song, Take My Hand, Precious Lord, he blamed himself for not being home the night his wife went into labor with their child, a son. Thomas had earlier told her he must go to church that particular night on important business and she had asked him to stay home. He assured her that he would not be long, but while he was away she went into labor and was taken to the hospital where she gave birth to a little boy. Shortly after giving birth she died and then a few hours later, the baby boy also died. Thomas blamed himself for not being there when his wife needed him the most. He was a broken man, checking himself into a mental hospital and one day while there, he sat down at the piano and wrote the song, "Precious Lord, Take My Hand and Lead Me On, And Help Me Stand, Through The Dark And Through The Night, Lead Me On To The Right". God touched Thomas's soul, a broken man who had all but given up on life, and He placed these words on Thomas's heart enabling him to put pen to paper and share these beautiful words of comfort with so many others, words that are still being sung today all over the world. Sometimes God lifts us up in our darkest hours and gives us strength to do our finest works. As Christians we are never alone, not even in our darkest hours because God will be there, lifting us. We have to be available to Him in order for Him to do this. We must not withdraw and expect God to do everything for us. God is ever present. He is not the one who goes away, rather it is us. We sometimes withdraw into ourselves, blaming others or even sometimes blaming God when things are not going smoothly in our lives.

Forgiveness

Do not beat yourself up because of your past. Lift yourself up for a righteous future. Bury yesterday, live righteously for today and rejoice for tomorrow.

Poet Henry Wadsworth Longfellow

On Christmas Day 1863 poet Longfellow wrote, with a heavy heart full of despair the carol, I Heard The Bells On Christmas Day based on the 1863 poem Christmas Bells. Just two years earlier Longfellow's personal life was shaken to its core when his devoted wife of 18 years dress caught on fire. He rushed to her aid and tried to extinguish the flames the best he could. He even used his own body trying to smother the flames. After suffering from severe burns, his beloved wife died on the following day, July 10, 1861. Because of Longfellow's attempt to save his wife's life he suffered severe facial burns. His wounds were so bad the grieving man was unable to attend his wife's funeral. He grew a beard to hide his egregiously scarred face and he worried that his deep, despairing grief might cause him to be locked away in an asylum. Longfellow's oldest son, Charley, the elder of six children and very much against his father's will, left his father's Massachusetts home and joined the Union Army. Young Charley became a second Lieutenant in the 1st Massachusetts Cavalry, missing the Battle of Gettysburg because of sickness from Typhoid Fever. After rejoining his unit on August 15, 1863 Henry Longfellow received a telegram dated November 27, 1863 informing him his son had been wounded in the battle of Mine Run campaign. Charley had been shot in the left shoulder and missed being paralyzed for life by less than an inch, a very close call. But, after a long healing period young Charley recovered and the war was over for him. A few months later, on Christmas Day 1863 is when Longfellow wrote his poem while war was raging all about him. Henry Longfellow, the 57 year old widowed poet and father of six children, in the midst of the deepest and darkest despair of his life and building from the sadness and violence engulfing his life, wrote the poem that would become a hauntingly beautiful and poignant Christmas Carol. This song is somewhat of an anthem for anyone who is troubled because it acknowledges the sorrow of life events and then brings full circle how God comforts and strengthens us even when we feel hopeless, the wrong shall fail the right will indeed prevail. When we become weak and weary and find ourselves in the midst of bleak despair, we must seek comfort knowing the Lord is our shepherd and will never leave us nor forsake us when we are in trials and troubles. The Lord is our shield, strength and salvation. He can and does give us some of our most enduring works when we are at our lowest ebb. If we keep God as our foundation always, we can inspire others using our spiritual gifts which in turn blesses us to do amazing things with renewed strength.

Part Four

Testimony

Many worshipers in today's churches just do not believe it is possible to communicate or have any personal encounters with God. Testimonies are extremely important and are incredible blessings to all church families as many find refuge and strength when others tell of their walk with God. Many followers have shared their stories of the healing power of God from illnesses and disease. Their testimonies are treasured blessings that bear much good fruit. Worshipers today struggle to realize that God is extremely supernatural in power. He can be anywhere at anytime and is everywhere all the time, a concept so vast it is very nearly impossible for our finite minds to grasp, and this is of course, where faith comes into being. God has many different ways to communicate with us and to manifest himself in our lives. God tells us over and over again in scriptures to listen for His voice and to look for signs of His second coming. Even our Vice President, Mike Pence has heard God's voice, maintaining that God speaks to him, and when God speaks directly to you, you will be the only one to hear His voice, even if you are in a room full of others. These experiences carry much power, and it is my feeling that half the people over the age of fifty have probably had at least one supernatural encounter in their lifetime. Yet, they are oftentimes silent because to mention such things opens one up to ridicule and disbelief, or worse yet, being thought of as a liar and maybe considered to be unstable to boot. I myself understand this feeling, this fear of being shamed for sharing experiences that don't seem to make sense to those who have no perception or experience themselves with anything supernatural. It is difficult for the naysayers to understand since they have no personal events to draw from. After my first book came out, Behind The Glass Door, people asked me how the book was doing and is it a success? I don't hesitate to tell them that yes, it is a success. I am the first to admit that the book is very strange and I realized when writing it that many people would find certain subjects difficult to be believed. Furthermore, the reason I tell people my book was a huge success is because I know I was obedient to God in doing what He told me to do. What shocked me about my book is that later on some readers of the book approached me and asked if I would listen to their supernatural encounters with God. Many of these people I have known for decades and there is no doubt about their honesty and sincerity. These stories of theirs contain miracles and make life more meaningful for all of us when shared. Every time someone comes forward to share one of their personal stories, I feel as if I have found a long lost friend. God is still performing amazingly beautiful miracles, you've only to open your ears and your eyes and your heart to witness; if you look for Him you will find Him. He is always here, he never leaves us, it is we who step away at times. God asked me to write the book, He instructed me actually, to attest for Him. God wants His people to know He is very much alive and powerful and He is working in our lives. Many Christians believe that when Jesus ascended into Heaven to be with His Father that all miracles ceased to exist. Nothing could be further from the truth, there are miracles every day, and He is the source of all life which is in and of itself miraculous. I've often talked about the beauty of Jesus and how impossible it is to describe such beauty because **there is nothing on Earth that compares to His amazing beauty.**

Testimony

Strange encounters with the supernatural are not all that uncommon as many people believe that God does not like being ignored and He can change your life course as quickly as a blinding light. The truth is that God has total control of our lives. He is in control. Never us. At thirteen years of age I felt I had total control of my young life until one night sitting alone in the back seat of an uncle's car I had my own very personal supernatural experience, (my wife says it was "my come to Jesus meeting", if you will). This event had happened while traveling to an out of town high school football game, while I had been minding my own business in the backseat of that uncle's car, we were just a few miles from our destination when our car entered a railroad underpass and God took over my life and my aunt and uncle in the front seat never knew what was going on with me. That their young nephew was experiencing a vision which appeared in a blinding flash of light, a nanosecond in today's terminology, as the car passed through the short under trestle tunnel. A vision of a car wreck some 50 miles away and and six hours into the future took place before my very incredulous eyes. I literally "saw" my brother and two of his closest friends in a car wreck that was bad enough they could have all been killed. It is a miracle they were not killed because it was that awful. This makes the point further that miracles happen every day, we should all be diligent and grateful for God's grace and mercy. The actual, physical wreck did happen at about 1 o'clock a.m. that certain Saturday morning of October 23, 1965. After my vision God taught me a valuable lesson, that He is in total control and that I should not (we should not) ever think differently. I will never grow tired of or disenchanted by others' personal supernatural experiences which lie outside the realm of science and its skepticism of same. Strange experiences are much more common than people realize, even in a community as small as my hometown of Lexington, Texas. One such story is about a family in Lexington who had relatives coming for a visit over the weekend. When the visiting woman woke up on Sunday morning she was most upset by a dream she had had during the night. She related that during the dream she was killed in a car wreck on their way home from this trip. Of course everyone comforted her, saying it was only a bad dream and she should not worry about such a thing. A few hours later this woman and her family departed for their home in Houston. Sometime later the host family would receive a telephone call informing them that the family had been involved in a terrible car accident and the woman had been killed. The woman's dream had come true, she had indeed perished in a car wreck on the way home. I know from my own experience that some dreams which are particularly strong and clear do have value and should never be ignored. Then another acquaintance of mine related that she had gotten up from her bed one night and upon entering her kitchen to get a glass of water, when there at the kitchen table as plain as day, sat her father in law. The man had been dead for many years! Truth is stranger than fiction and that is the truth! More recently, a lady I know who lives a few miles outside Lexington, put her near death experience on the Internet as a testimony to others. I am very proud of her bravery in doing this as I know how hard it can be to put oneself "out there in the wide open" for some to gainsay or ridicule. Anyway, in her testimony she spoke of very bright lights and the unfathomable beauty of Heaven and the angels. And like many others who experience NDE's she did not want to return to her earthly body. Because of this event she absolutely knows there is a Heaven and that death is really a rebirth.

While waiting for a family member at the Veterans' Hospital in Temple, Texas a minister I spoke with told me that when he was young and a member of the U.S. Coastguard, his stomach had burst. He had actually died in the emergency room and remembered going to Heaven, but was sent back because in Heaven he was told that it was not yet his time. On yet another occasion, and this was in Elgin, Texas, I was attending a talk from a man who had a NDE. He spoke about dying and waking up in Heaven flat on his back in the middle of a dirt road. He said he heard a loud wind-noise as though many birds were whooshing their wings in the sky, and upon looking closer he indeed saw what looked like birds coming to the ground. But as they approached he realized they were not birds at all, but rather they were all angels, surrounding him within a bright circle of light. He claimed he could see a hand entering this light circle and then a voice told him that he must go back as it was not yet his time and that he should not worry because he would have help when he returned. Upon awakening in the hospital, it so happened that every night a male nurse, a rather large man, came into his room and rubbed oil on his legs until he healed. He repeatedly told all who would listen of this man who had helped his poor legs to heal but no one knew what he was talking about. When he spoke of the nurse coming into his room rubbing this oil on his legs, no one at the hospital knew of a nurse like this, or even of a nurse fitting this description. One never knows just where or when one will have such an experience, or even if one will ever have such a preview of eventual eternity, for everyone doesn't get to experience this phenomenon.

One day my wife, Jeanie and I traveled to Milano, Texas to watch one of our granddaughters play in a volleyball game. A woman we know from the Thrall, Texas area had come to watch her granddaughter as well, and she sat down beside me and we began talking. She told me she had read my book **Behind The Glass Door** and enjoyed it because she strongly felt that she also had received an experience from God. She related that her unique experience came to her when she was having a difficult time and had been a little depressed. Continuing, she told me she had gone to Taylor, Texas to a fast food restaurant to eat and as she sat alone focusing on her plate she felt a strange presence. So, in looking up she saw a tall, pleasant-looking man dressed in pure white clothing peering down at her, then he smiled and walked away. At the time, she couldn't help but feel that he just seemed so out of place there and that their brief interchange was rather unusual and maybe a bit unsettling, though not in the least scary. She finished her meal and went out to her car readying to leave the parking lot when she again noticed the same man, all dressed in white standing by her driver's side car window. My friend explained to me that she did not feel the least bit threatened or frightened by his presence, so she put her window down and the man told her he could not help but notice that she seemed troubled by something. He then asked her if she would allow him to pray for her, to which she agreed. She said that the man in white prayed the most beautiful prayer she had ever heard in her entire life. Then he smiled and told her, "I hope you feel better". Then he simply walked away. She told me she had no idea who that man was, and that maybe that is just the way it is supposed to be, but at the same time she really wasn't sure "what" he was, either. That experience so lifted her spirits that she went straight away to a nursing home and volunteered to visit those patients who were lonely and needed companionship, a practice she continues to this day.

I wanted to include these foregoing stories because it seems that very few in our society like to talk about death, it seems at times a taboo subject most like to avoid lest they have to come to terms with their own mortality or because they do not want to be thought of as morbid and unpleasant. But many people who have had NDE's are anything but unpleasant or morbid, rather they are well-balanced and stable individuals whom God chose to give a glimpse of Heaven. It is my belief that God desires for these folks to "come back" and share their knowledge with the world, as some claim their NDE was like a fascinating homecoming and they proudly speak of their new spiritual body that is much like the earthly body except it's weightless and perfect. How wonderful will that be! Seeing the beauty of Jesus and visiting Heaven is a special gift that changes peoples' lives and their views about life, and death as it were. These people come back knowing they will someday return to paradise and therefore they have less fear concerning death because of their experiences with eternity. Just maybe the old saying about what doesn't kill you only makes you stronger...is true.

Stand Up For God

Some few years ago my wife and I were invited to Bastrop to hear a man give a speech about a moment in History involving his elderly father in Hitler's Germany. The speech was really very good and afterward some of us were invited to attend lunch at a local restaurant. My wife and I sat across the table from the speaker who was seated beside his young twenty-something daughter. We enjoyed a nice meal together and as we visited he began to share about his church and how he served as an active member in his church. As we conversed, we couldn't help noticing that he casually took the Lord's name on at least two occasions, seemingly not even realizing he had done so. I found it difficult to believe he had taken God's name in vain without so much as blinking an eye. I really do not believe he even realized he had done so, it had become such a habit. I have known this man most of my life albeit at a distance. I know he comes from a good family and that he is in his heart a good man. I felt then I should say something like, "do you know you just took God's name in vain?" But, we were sitting at a table full of people and I didn't want to embarrass him and his daughter. I felt badly and very guilty for remaining silent. Thinking back I realized I should have asked him one simple question. My friend, if you are crossing a street and you forgot to look before crossing and a car is coming at you and then a complete stranger runs out into the street and at the very last possible second snatches you from certain death, but that person in turn is then hit by the car and lying dead in the street, having sacrificed his life for yours. If you could say anything to this man, what is the one thing you would say to him? I feel sure you would thank him and praise him for saving your life. I know you would not curse his name with shame after he died for you. God gave His son to die a painful death on the cross for you and for me. So please choose your words more carefully because I know you are a better man than to do otherwise.

Stand Up For Christ

On September 16, 2017 my wife, Jeanie and I decided to take a one day road trip just to get out of the house. It was a beautiful day and we stopped not too far from our home and visited a local antique shop in Paige, Texas. Anxious to see what hidden treasures we might uncover, we entered the establishment and promptly encountered a vendor, one of many in this quite large store. This particular man happened to have a very large picture of Jesus presented in a glass frame. Asking if I could hold it and take a closer look, he handed me the picture. As I passed the picture back to the owner he grinned and said, "Jesus looks good for someone who has been dead forever", to which I did not say a word. Exiting the store my wife and I decided to continue our trip and headed into Bastrop for some lunch. But driving away from the store I began to realize something. I realized that I was actually very upset at the words spoken by the man back at the antiques shop. Had he really said that Jesus was dead? I was not so much upset with him as I was with myself, for missing an opportunity to tell that man what the truth is, that Jesus is not dead, but that he is so beautiful and strong and very much alive! That Jesus has lived for more than two thousand years and has only known 3 days of death. Jesus was born to a young, virgin mother and came to save us all from sin. And that it was Jesus' purpose to come to Earth and die on the cross. I felt I should have told the man the truth, that no one who has ever walked on Earth is more alive than Jesus Christ.

Our Savior is more alive today than at any other time. He is still with us, and with all who seek Him. Jeremiah 29: 13 "You will find me when you seek me, if you look for me in earnest."

A Good, Though Misguided Friend

One night while celebrating my wife's birthday with close friends, a good man that I have known for years asked me an unusual question that totally caught me off guard. He said, "David, do you think heaven will be a boring place? Because all you do all day is sit on a cloud playing a harp?" With great difficulty I stopped myself from laughing because I realized he was only half joking, meaning the other half was a serious question. So I carefully thought for a few seconds before answering him, then I told my friend, "your brother is the lead singer in a band that is so good they play tours around the world, and I know how much you yourself love music, right? So I believe that when you die the first night you're in heaven, Elvis will be on stage singing his heart out, and on another stage maybe soul singer Marvin Gaye will be singing *Brother, Brother*, and maybe for country and western lovers old Hank Williams, Sr. will be singing *I Saw The Light*. And if you tire of listening to music maybe you can take art lessons from the Masters, like French Impressionist Claude Monet or Spanish Surrealist Salvador Dali or the great Dutch painter and portraitist, Rembrandt. Or you could attend lectures by great people of history, down through all the ages such as Washington, Napoleon, Churchill and one of the greatest of all, Joan of Arc, the holy warrior who saved France from an invading English army, as a 13 year old peasant girl who was anointed by God to save France. I then told my friend to just imagine all the good and great people that will be in God's

Kingdom, so how could anyone become bored in Heaven? I further explained that everyone who lives on this earth must die, but in Heaven life is eternal and not one thing dies in Heaven. The environment in Heaven will be perfect, the air and water will be fresh, and we will be instantly mesmerized by the perfect beauty surrounding us. It may be much like Earth, except that everything will be perfectly clean, I can only imagine the many kinds of plant life and species of animals. The trees will be full of birds of beautiful colors singing songs and praising God. Suddenly you may notice your formerly old sickly and worn out body has been replaced by a new spiritual body, a body built for eternity. Now when you walk it will feel as if you are walking on air. I told him I believe our new bodies will be similar to our old earthly bodies but that it will be in good ways because the heavenly bodies will have no limitations and never feel pain or suffering, and aging will simply no longer exist as we will live forever. Heaven will only be full of good people from all different nations, tribes and religions, having arrived there for one reason and that is their love for Christ. Everyone will be perfectly equal, not one judged by their wealth, their physicality or their skin color. I then told my friend that although I have never seen Heaven, that I have witnessed the beauty of Jesus and that I well and truly can imagine Heaven, where we will live only to love and praise God and to be beloved by God. Also admonishing my dear friend to cast away his worries, because Heaven, oh no, Heaven will not be boring, I can promise you this.

Part Five

Job

One of my favorite bible stories is the book of Job. He was a good man who always kept a safe distance from evil and God blessed him with a large family of seven sons and three daughters. Job was the wealthiest man in the entire area, owning as many as 2,000 sheep, 3,000 camels, 500 oxen teams and 500 female donkeys. And because of the vast amount of livestock owned, he employed many loyal servants to tend to his great herds. One day Satan came to the Lord and the Lord asked Satan where have you come from? Satan replied that he had been looking around on Earth, to which the Lord queried Satan, asking did you happen to notice my loyal servant, Job who loves me and will have nothing to do with sin? Satan scoffed at the Lord, why shouldn't he love you, you give him everything he asks for! You protect his home, family and property from all harm. Satan then said the Lord had spoiled Job and why doesn't he [the Lord] just try taking everything away that he dearly loves, then he will curse you to your face! The Lord replied to Satan that he could try Job, but that he was not to harm him physically. Oh, and there are so many ways to harm someone other than physically. So just as soon as Satan left the Lord's presence he set to work on Job's life. Of course, Job had no way of knowing the complete hell and suffering Satan was preparing to unleash on his life. Job's sons and daughters were dining at the oldest brother's house when Satan caused a mighty wind to form and this mighty wind destroyed the house and killed every one of Job's children. A servant who had survived told Job of the terrible tragedy. Job tore his robe from his body in grief, crying out that he had come into this world with nothing and that he would die with nothing, that the Lord had been good to him and everything he had lost was given to him by God, they were his [God's] to take away. Then Job was told by his only surviving servant that all his herds had been driven off or stolen and that not one remained. So quite literally, everything of any value Job had loved and cared for was completely gone in one day. These catastrophic events left Job a sick and broken man, with tremendous sorrow. But even still, throughout all this misery he did not turn against God, rather he continued to stand firm in his faith in God and to pray to God. Satan realized Job was not going to be easy to turn from the Lord, so Satan told the Lord he would make Job sick because a man will do anything to save his own flesh, and then he will surely curse you to your face! The Lord told Satan, do as you please with him but do not take his life. So Satan struck Job with painful boils from head to foot, and Job scraped the sores with a broken piece of pottery and rubbed ashes in the wounds, trying to attain some relief from this added misery. Job's wife told him just look what God has done to you, why don't you curse him before you die! But Job said no, I will not curse my Lord, you heathen woman! Then three of Job's closest friends came to him as soon as they heard of all the tragedies that had befallen him. They had come to comfort him but when they first saw him they could hardly recognize him he was so physically broken from grief and the affliction of boils. Even throughout all his sorrow and pain, Job held tightly onto his faith and love for the Lord. His loyal friends sat on the ground with him for seven days and seven nights in silence, knowing that words were not great enough to help this troubled shadow of a man. They hoped their presence there with him would give him some comfort. With a deep, weary,

Job

and depressed voice Job prayed to God and asked him what had happened to him that he would bring all this into his life? Job felt he was innocent of sin, that he always fed the hungry and helped the poor every chance he got. And he prayed with a pure heart reflecting how could his life come to such tragedies. He had never lied or deceived, his heart had never lusted after another man's wife, he had never been unfair to his servants, nor cursed anyone else or asked revenge against anyone. Saying he didn't know what he had done or what he should be doing, for if his God opposed him, what hope could there possibly be for his soul? Continuing to pray, he asked the Lord to please let him know if he had wronged Him. Then the most wonderful thing happened, the Lord accepted Job's prayer and restored his wealth by giving him twice the size herds he had before, along with twice as much land. He restored Job's health and again restored Job with seven sons and three daughters so that he once more found happiness in life and Job indeed continued to pray and to praise God for his renewed life. Job lived to the ripe old age of 140 years, living a good life and enjoying his many grandchildren and great grandchildren.

Salvation is not for sale. It can only be earned through faith in Christ. It is a gift from Christ ~

Lazarus

Throughout Jesus' three year ministry he often traveled to the village of Bethany. He met and became friends with Mary, Martha and their younger brother Lazarus. Most times they fed and gave Jesus a place to sleep as the young family enjoyed Jesus and were fascinated by his remarkable words of wisdom regarding the Gospel. Oftentimes they stayed awake into the early hours listening to the amazing stories shared by Jesus. They adored Jesus and always looked forward to his visits, and Jesus always felt at home with the small family and loved them very much. The two sisters loved their younger brother who was always helping others in the village, especially caring for the sick. One day after caring for the sick, Lazarus came home and told Martha he had been visiting others but that he actually was not feeling well himself. Lazarus took to his bed and as time passed he began feeling worse and running a high fever. Soon both his sisters became very worried and sent a trusted friend to find Jesus and ask him to please come quickly because Lazarus' condition was worsening all the time. The sisters knew Jesus couldn't have gone very far because he had just spent the previous night at their home. The messenger found Jesus and his disciples not too far down the road and appealed to Jesus to please come to Lazarus' rescue saying, *"Lord, behold, he whom thou lovest is sick"*, Jesus then told the man, *"this sickness is not unto death, but for the glory of God, that the son of God might be glorified thereby."* The man carried back these words from Jesus to the sisters. Lazarus was lying in bed dying and Jesus knew this, but still he was in no particular hurry to go to Lazarus' aid, not for several more days. The disciples were puzzled and did not understand Jesus' reluctance to help his beloved friend who was so clearly in danger, did Jesus not recognize the seriousness of the appeal for help? What Jesus knew was that Lazarus was already dead and so he was in no hurry to return. But, early on the fourth day Jesus told his disciples, *"our friend Lazarus sleepeth; but I go, that I may wake him out of sleep"*. Jesus' announcement surprised the disciples because they knew going back into Bethany, only a few miles from Jerusalem, was dangerous because earlier there had been an attempt on Jesus' life. Thomas boldly said to the others: "Let us also go, that we may die with him." But on that certain evening of the fourth day, Jesus and his disciples arrived at the outskirts of Bethany and according to custom for that time and place, families immediately buried their dead. So it was they found Lazarus's sisters in their home with friends gathered around trying to console them in their grief. Martha went outside her home and approached Jesus first, and with painful anguish in her voice she spoke to Jesus saying, *"Lord, if thou hadst been here, my brother would not have died."* Jesus tenderly told Martha, *"thy brother shall rise again."* Then Jesus said, *"I am the resurrection and the life: he that believeth in me, though he were dead, yet shall he live: and whosoever liveth and believeth in me, shall never die."* Martha went back inside and then soon after her sister, Mary came out and approached Jesus, and with her eyes brimming over with tears and her voice filled with pain asked her Lord, *"why didn't you come to Lazarus who so loved you, and save his life?"* Martha then went and stood with her sister Mary before Jesus and both sisters were overcome by deep sorrow and grief. Others gathered around the grieving sisters and soon the entire group was loudly wailing because in that village everyone had known and loved Lazarus. The sorrow Jesus witnessed deeply troubled him, and Jesus had begun to shed tears as well and he questioned them, *"where have you laid him?"* The sisters and the mourning crowd of friends led Jesus to the site of the tomb that had been sealed by a large stone. The body of Lazarus had been wrapped in a burial cloth and placed in the cave-like tomb for four days and the large stone closed the entrance. Jesus looked at the sealed tomb and turned and looked at his faithful disciples standing alongside the two grieving women and the large crowd that had gathered around to see Jesus and what he was doing. He then spoke to Martha and Mary and made them a promise that their brother shall rise again. The sisters thought Jesus was saying Lazarus would rise again in Heaven, but as we know now, they were about to receive the shock of their lives. Jesus asked several large, strong men to remove the stone blocking the entrance to the tomb. As the stone was removed a strong stench of death came from out of the tomb and the men scrambled away very quickly to escape the unpleasant odor of death. Then Jesus raised his hands toward Heaven and looked upward, and praying, asked his Father for the power and authority for the miracle he was to perform. Jesus suddenly lowered his hands and pointed to the tomb with his right hand, then he spoke loudly in a strong and commanding voice, *"Lazarus, rise, come forth."* (This writer feels it a very important point for readers to realize here. That when Jesus spoke, he did so *directly* to Lazarus, saying *Lazarus, rise and come forth.* Had Jesus not spoken to the individual of Lazarus, then there might well have been a so called "zombie fest", because had he not specified Lazarus by name, then ALL the dead interred in that common burial place would have risen and come forth.) When the Lord speaks, even those in death can hear his transcendent voice and obey his every command. Yes, the Lord has all authority and his amazing power conquers even death. Jesus said, "I am the resurrection". After a few moments Lazarus slowly came out of the burial tomb but his motion was limited because he was still wrapped tightly in his burial clothing. The people in the crowd were unprepared and shocked at what they had just witnessed, even as Jesus said to several standing close by to go to Lazarus, *"loose him and let him go."* Some of the astonished witnesses in the crowd were prominent Jews, who were unfriendly to Jesus and no matter how hard they tried to refuse him, they could not deny the blessed miracle they had just seen. Many of these unfriendly men went back to the temple to tell the high priests how Jesus had raised Lazarus from the dead and restored life back into his body. Lazarus rising from his tomb stands as the third recorded instance of restoration to life by Jesus. So in this story Jesus did not go immediately to aid Lazarus on his sick bed because Jesus wanted to heal him after death claimed him. Jesus used Lazarus' death as a valuable lesson for his disciples and all the onlookers to prove all the power and authority his Father gives him. Jesus can command the dead to rise and thereby conquer death. Because of the testimonies of those present who witnessed the raising of Lazarus, the Jewish priests became very angry and scared of losing their power forever to a miracle worker. They decided he must be taken into custody and silenced forever. Soon after the restoration of Lazarus' life, there was a large celebration feast in his honor. It was a joyful time for Jesus and the disciples, and the sisters were so happy to have their brother back from the dead. All gave praise to Jesus, the true Son of God. As soon as the celebration was over Jesus took his disciples and withdrew from Bethany into a village called Ephraim, a safe distance from Jerusalem. Jesus knew his time on Earth was nearing an end and with time running out he still had much to teach his twelve followers to prepare them to continue his ministry for when he left to go be with his father. The next several months they would spend listening and learning his Father's ways and words. After which they would go back to Jerusalem and the cross.

Paul
Paul's Remarkable Journey

Saul, the son of a devout Jew, was proud of his pure Jewish blood. Being a Hebrew born of Hebrews, his original name was Saul. He was a member of the Benjamin Tribe and was very aware of his Jewish religious and cultural heritage. Saul was highly educated in Greek culture and in his Roman faith. Saul hardly looked the part of a man that was to become a legend. He was short of stature, bow-legged, hook-nosed and bald-headed, but was described to be amazingly, physically strong. Saul adamantly felt he was serving God by arresting and persecuting Jesus' followers, and so it was that Saul was present when Stephen was publicly stoned to death and he was filled with a fanatical determination to defend the honor of God and to destroy this heresy. Saul was commissioned to travel north on the Damascus Road and arrest any followers he could find. Just a few miles from the city, a blinding light from Heaven struck Saul and he fell to his knees, blinded and confused. Next he heard a voice coming down from Heaven, (heard only by Saul because God was speaking directly to Saul). *"Saul, Saul, why do you persecute me? I am Jesus, whom you are persecuting...Rise, and go back to the city, and you will be told what to do."* With the help of his traveling companions, a spiritually awakened Saul was led back to Damascus. Saul sat in a dark room for three days tended to by his friends. He prayed and wondered about his future and was very, very confused by his experience.

Jesus instructed his loyal Christian disciple, Ananias to go to Saul and baptize him with the Holy Spirit, and then to unfold and complete the divine commission of the apostle to the Gentiles. After Saul was baptized the scales of blindness fell from his eyes and the world was a new world to him because he was no longer Saul, for now he was a new Christian, known as Paul. Paul's acceptance of Jesus as the Messiah was different than that of the other apostles in that they had walked with Jesus for more than three years. Jesus had been their teacher, and they witnessed miracles, they had loyally followed him and served him with love and they shared their beautiful memories with Paul. Actually, Paul probably never laid eyes on Jesus in the flesh, but Paul understood that Jesus raised him up to serve. In a mere thirty-seven years after the crucifixion of Christ Paul helped to create a worldwide church and bring Christianity to all Gentiles. Paul's shattering experience on the road to Damascus gave him a unique and personal faith. Paul's conversion was a total reversal from his old misguided life. Paul baptized and nourished multitudes of people by the Holy Spirit of Christ. After Paul's divine conversion he became a close member of Jesus' disciples. He became a man of two worlds, as Paul's old friends who were Pharisees, rejected him and persecuted him to the end of his life, but his new, elite disciple-friends thoroughly educated Paul about their personal experiences with Jesus. Paul became the most influential apostle of the New Testament period, he became chief missionary to the Gentiles and his early gospel teachings turned the world upside down. Paul was aware that he was led by the Holy Spirit to preach and to establish churches around the world. He laid hands on the sick and healed them, and the Holy Spirit came into them. Paul expressed the importance of water baptism and felt that there was a mystical union with Christ at baptism which made a person a "new person" and proclaiming that baptism removes our sins. Thusly, we are "born again". He continually preached the importance of prayer, saying, "Let your request be made known to God," and to "Pray constantly, give thanks in all circumstances." Paul realized he was a born again person filled with the Holy Spirit. *"It is no longer I who live but Christ who lives in me."* He knew that *"where your treasure is, there will your heart be also."* He became a great example of courage, his conquests of fear and faith made him one of the greatest missionaries of the First Century. Paul's conversion is one of the greatest stories of salvation there has ever been. By the grace of God, Paul was born again and given a second chance at life so he could loyally serve God the remainder of his life. He traveled to places around the world and this great and determined man of God was one of the world's first establishers of churches in the world. Apostle Paul had many different traveling companions as he journeyed the world from Asia, Spain and Italy (Rome). During this time a shy, very timid young man called Timothy, became especially close to Paul and served him as a disciple running difficult errands for Paul. Timothy was under no illusions as to the cost and danger of his discipleship to Paul, and Paul loved the gentle young man as a son. Timothy acted as Paul's secretary and Paul's letters to Timothy were well recorded. Paul wrote about hardships in II Corinthians 11 :23-28. With far greater labors [than other apostles], far more imprisonments, and even with countless beatings to the point of near-death, Paul said that five times he had received at the hands of the Jews the forty lashes less one. Three times he was beaten with rods and once he was stoned. Three times he was shipwrecked; and for a night and a day he was adrift at sea. And on frequent journeys he was in danger from rivers, and robbers, and from his own people as well as the Gentiles. There was danger in the cities, in the wildernesses, on the seas, and danger from false brethren; in toil and hardships through many a sleepless night, he lay in hunger and thirst, as he was so often without food, in cold and exposure to the elements. And apart from these things there was daily pressure upon him because of his anxiety for all the churches and his letters provided a genuine accounting of his dangerous travels. Paul focused much of his attention on the life, teachings, death and resurrection of Jesus Christ. He did not try to neglect the passages of the Old Testament, rather he focused more on his religious experiences through Christ. Paul did quote a reference to God's forgiveness in Psalms 32:1-2 ~ *"Blessed is the man against whom the Lord will not reckon his sin"*. God is always ready to forgive, Jesus promised the comfort and mercy of God. God's promise, unless we *"turn and become like children"*, we shall not see the kingdom of Heaven. God taught Paul the reality of repentance and forgiveness on the road to Damascus, this "single act" of being blinded by the light was a true realization of the facts and nature of Saul's sins. He faced the awful seriousness of his sins but found a depth and quality of repentance from his born again experience. No doubt Paul's contact with the risen Christ was a spiritual gift. Saul persecuted the church of God violently and tried to destroy it, but Paul said, *"I was born again by the grace of God."* Paul's life was lived in the midst of conflict but there was and there can be no doubt that he was loved by many who stood firmly and loyally by him. Paul left behind him a treasure of written letters from his own hand whereas Jesus did not. These primitive letters are excellent sources left for us to receive a religious history from the late first century and are a reconstruction of the life of

Jesus from birth to death, giving a firsthand look at the early authenticity of Jesus' teachings. One of Paul's most superior gifts was his closeness to Jesus' disciples who had witnessed his life and ministry all the way to his resurrection. Paul's letters made a distinct contribution to the writing of the scriptures. Paul said, *"I persecuted the church of God. But by the grace of God I am what I am, and His grace toward me is not in vain. I tried to destroy the church but I was reborn through his grace."* Paul became the great builder of the church. He traveled and established churches around the world, attending to their pastors and administering duties. He was both a great evangelist and apostle, and made a huge contribution to the church, often using different titles for the church members, calling them *members of the family of God*, and *the church is the bride of Christ*, and we are *a colony of Heaven*. Christianity has a message for all the world - it is clearly the message meant for all the people of the world.

Note: Shortly after Jesus' resurrection he appeared to his eleven remaining disciples and told them, *"I have been given all authority in heaven and on earth. Go therefore and make disciples of all nations, baptizing them in the name of the Father and of the Son and of the Holy Spirit, teaching them to observe all that I have commanded you. And behold, I am with you always, to the end of the age."* Matthew 28:18-20

Moses

I understand that I am referring back to the Old Testament in writing about Moses, but he was such an important figure in the history of the world and of the Bible itself, that I feel compelled to share the following:

Moses is the most majestic figure in the Old Testament. No one had a closer relationship with God than Moses, and God spoke often to Moses. In the story of Moses, Pharaoh's daughter came down to the river to bathe and found a baby floating in a basket among the bulrushes After which she got a Hebrew nurse to suckle the child until he had grown big enough to wean from the breast. She adopted this little baby whom she named Moses and he grew up as an Egyptian surrounded by great wealth while remaining aware of his Hebrew origins. Years later in his adulthood, God commanded Moses to lead his brethren out of their oppression and into the Promised Land. Moses pointed out to God that he was slow of speech and of tongue and might not be the best orator for God's purposes. So then God instructed Moses to let his brother Aaron be his spokesman. For forty years Moses, along with his brother, Aaron wandered in the wilderness leading the Israelites to the Promised Land. While in the wilderness God called Moses to Mount Sinai to receive The Ten Commandments and God spoke to Moses on the mountain, *"I am the Lord your God who brought you out of the land of Egypt out of the house of bondage. You shall have no other Gods before me."* When Moses came down from the mountain with two tablets of stone written with the finger of God, he could not believe his eyes. Those left in the care of Aaron had melted their gold jewelry and molded a golden calf, and they were feasting and dancing naked around it. Moses, in a blind rage, threw the tablets to the ground breaking them into pieces. He then threw the golden calf into a fire and after it melted he mixed water with the molten gold and forced some of the Israelites to swallow it. In a continuing rage Moses upbraided his brother Aaron, who tried to defend himself telling Moses, *"you know the people, that they are set on evil"*. So Moses ordered a large number of idol-worshippers put to the sword. This painful experience deeply troubled Moses, leaving him with a sense of failure. Moses asked God to relieve him of leadership but God told Moses to continue on for the end of the journey was nearing. Before continuing the journey Moses went back to the sacred mountain and received the new tablets engraved in stone, The Ten Commandments. When Moses descended the mountain with the new tablets the Israelites became scared of him and refused to go near him because his face shone with light. God told Moses to build an ark to carry the tablets and that it would be used as a portable Temple for the wandering Israelites. The Lord gave Moses precise instructions that this ark should be built to certain cubits in length, breadth, and height and with wood covered entirely in gold. The ark was constructed as per God's command. Wearily, Moses asked God to choose a new leader to take the people into The Promised Land. The Lord chose Joshua, "a man in whom is the Spirit". Moses did not go into The Promised Land, but God let him see it from the top of Mount Nebo. At a hundred and twenty years old Moses died, and the Lord buried him in a valley in the land of Moab. When news of Moses's death reached his people they wept and mourned for thirty days for the great leader and teacher they had lost, for they knew that no man had known the Lord better than Moses had. More than thirty-five hundred years ago Moses chose his path when he renounced his right to the throne of Egypt and decided to follow his faith in God. Moses was forty years old when he made this great decision. As the adopted son of Pharaoh's daughter, he lived a privileged life allowing him every kind of luxury, he was an educated man who chose God over wealth and power. By faith he forsook Egypt, not fearing the wrath of the king, Moses chose the path of God because he understood the rewards of following God, which were far greater than all the wealth of Egypt. Moses was neither weak minded nor weak willed and when Moses chose his faith he burned all bridges behind him. Moses was not a man of fear, he wholeheartedly turned his life over to God forever by faith. He surrendered his old life for a new life of devotion. Moses chose the narrow path, the more difficult path and he understood there would be many trials and much suffering and many more hardships along the way. But because of his strong faith, at the end of the path he recognized the triumphs and the rewards of eternal life. Few men have ever given up as much for God as Moses did. Moses's great sacrifice would lead to a greater reward. He was the envy of every man of his time and gave it all up to follow God's plan, [he that diligently seeks God is rewarded]. The Bible teaches that faith pleases God more than anything else, *"without faith it is impossible to please him"*. The Bible declares faith is absolutely essential and that salvation comes only through faith. *"Believe on the Lord Jesus Christ, and thou shalt be saved and thy house."* We are saved by grace through faith and we must all acknowledge that we are sinners and that Christ died on the cross because of us [our sinfulness]. All Christians have a duty to study our Bibles and learn the grace and salvation of Christ.

People today ask the same question the disciples asked Jesus, how much faith does it take? Jesus said, *"only the faith of a grain of mustard seed."* When we read our Bibles we will find many answers to difficult things in everyday life. In faith comes a better life and attitude, for the Bible is full of amazing facts and answers for everything that happens in life. Our heavenly Father provided us everything we need to get along in this life, it is in His divine instruction book, The Holy Bible. Moses renounced the wealth of Egypt because there was an emptiness in his life which all the wealth of Egypt could not fill. Moses understood the true wealth of the world was his faith in God, and he wanted to serve and please God. The same is true for us, and no matter how hopeless our future seems there is always the helping hand of Christ to lift us up. Only when we let go of our lives can we then become born anew. Like Moses, when we have saving faith in God, (for us it is God in the form of His son, Jesus Christ whom we accept as our personal Savior) then we have taken the final step toward having complete peace and joy in knowing we will have eternal life. We have found our path.

Pharisees

One Sunday Jesus was invited to the home of a prominent Pharisee. There were other guests present and one of them was a man afflicted with dropsy (in today's terminology he may have been suffering the effects of edema due to congestive heart failure). Jesus realized that these people were tempting him to heal this man, to use the Lord's power on the Sabbath. Pharisees' law prohibited any kind of work on the Sabbath, even a healing miracle. Jesus spoke to the Pharisees saying, *"Is it lawful to heal on the Sabbath?"* No one answered Jesus' question, but then Jesus placed his hand on the sick man and healed him. Jesus turned and asked the people assembled there in that room, *"If one of you had an ass or ox fall into a pit would you not pull him out on the Sabbath day?"* The astonished guests remained prudently silent. Guests attending the Pharisees' dinner were officials, lawyers, famous Rabbis and renowned scholars, all men of prominence. Before Jesus sat down at the table to feast he surprised everyone by blessing the meal before them. Jesus felt concern and a certain sadness for the others at the table, knowing they were spiritually sickly and living in evil ways as they were lovers of money and power, often using unrighteous business practices rife with deceit and trickery. Most were both dishonest and very crafty, but were living in self-denial and viewed themselves as honest and straightforward. Sadly, Jesus saw these men as they truly were, as men who had grown arrogantly proud of their sinfully chosen lifestyle. Jesus felt a deep concern for these men and their evil ways and began telling them a story about a shepherd whose flock had gone astray. Because of the shepherd's love for his flock, he desired to search and find the lost ones, leading them back into the safety of the fold. Whenever the shepherd found a strayed sheep, he did not punish it but rather he rejoiced, carrying it back to the fold on his shoulders and telling others to rejoice with him, for he had found his sheep which was lost! Jesus directed this parable to those spiritually sick men seated with him at the table in this way, *"I say unto you, that likewise joy shall be in Heaven over one sinner that asks repentance."* Jesus was explaining to these men the need for repentance, and the love, joy and reward for those recovered from spiritual corruption. Jesus ministered to those gathered there about lost and regained souls and the cleansing of their sins explaining that the loss of a soul is very sad and painful, and that it is Jesus' will that not one should perish, but that every soul is precious in the eyes of God.

Prophets

God has various ways of communicating with people and in ancient times God spoke directly to the great spiritual leaders of Israel. He made his ways known unto Moses, *"and the Lord spake unto Moses face to face"*. Most of the prophets and seers felt that they had received direct, unique, unmistakable messages directly from God. Albeit, some tried to refuse or resist, but eventually they became obedient. No one can volunteer to become a prophet regardless of their relationship with God, only selected individuals chosen directly by God become prophets and seers, and they do not think of themselves as creative individuals, but rather as obedient people to whom God has revealed himself to in many different and unique ways. Often, prophets have conflict with a doubtful society. Many times God speaks to his prophets through his divine voice, making his will known. These prophets commissioned to receive God's voice are very aware of God and his activity in the world, having a divine guidance and maturity to receive such revelations from God. Ancient Native American Indians called their prophets medicine men, or "Holy men", with strong medicine. It is difficult for ordinary people to acknowledge and understand the relationship God has with his prophets. The Old Testament is filled with references to angels who made God's purposes known to men. Angels are God's messengers who eagerly serve him. God's revelations can also be revealed in dreams and visions. As in 1 Samuel 28:6 ~ When Saul saw the great army of Philistines he became frantic with fear, and he asked God what they should do. The Lord refused to answer him either by dream or by vision or by prophets ~ Every prophet knows and understands the amazing voice of God. Every word from God has pinpoint accuracy that goes directly to the core of the soul. God does not waste words and he can speak volumes by only uttering a few words. The voice of God is the most reassuring voice there is, rife with wisdom. When God tells you to do something you will believe him and you will fulfill his command with divine faith. You will hear the pure truth in his beautiful voice and become empowered by the Holy Spirit. God's voice is sharper than any two edged sword and he has ways of making his will known to the ordinary man with a special measure of divine power and direction. God directly guided Peter with a vision. The Spirit said unto him, *"behold, three men seek thee, arise then, and get thee down, and go with them, doubting nothing, for I have sent them."* God's spirit is always actively working. Bible scholars recognize the importance of prophecies and the value of dreams and visions. One night King Nebuchadnezzar had a mysterious dream about a large metallic man made of four different metals (Daniel 2:31-35) Daniel interpreted the dream for the king, stating the head is gold, the chest and the arms represent silver, the third and fourth metals bronze and iron. The four metals represent the successive kingdom of Babylon. Great prophets provide key details with definite answers, prophecies made many centuries ago are coming true today before our eyes. Just a few years ago, Isis fighters tortured and murdered Christians because of their faith; those innocents were martyrs, and the prophets had forewarned of Christians' persecution. Knowledge is key to life, but sadly there will always be those who doubt and will be full of unbelief and sarcasm. What you do not know, you cannot believe and what you do not believe, that is why you cannot release your faith. Believers filled with the Holy Spirit are carriers of the power of God. When a person is anointed by God they are given God's resources and supernatural abilities and can, therefore, accomplish anything. 1 Corinthians 12:4-11 says God gives us many kinds of special gifts and abilities, and there are many different ways to serve God. There are also many ways in which God works in our lives as well. The Holy Spirit displays God's power through each of us, to one he gives special faith, and to another he gives the power to heal the sick. He can give power for doing miracles to some, and to others the power to prophesy and preach. It is the Holy Spirit who gives all these gifts and powers, deciding which gift each one of us should have. All prophets are hand chosen by God. They are anointed to serve. God is believed to have a plan for every life. God's plan for man's existence fits in with the larger strategy of building that community of guided spirits which Christ calls Heaven. One of the Lord's most mysterious and powerful prophets first mentioned about the year 865 B.C., was Elijah. Not much is known about this mysterious man's background, but he became a soldier of the Lord and fought against heathen gods. He had a personal relationship with God and was allowed to perform mighty miracles. Elisha witnessed Elijah being taken up to Heaven by a chariot of fire, like a whirlwind he disappeared from sight to be with his Lord. By Jewish tradition, Elijah has not died, and continues to wander Earth. He will reappear to usher in the Messiah and the final redemption of mankind. Today God is still using men and women as human agents to work miracles, but miracles today are not on the same level and power as those implemented by Moses, Elijah or Jesus. So far, modern-day Christians are still operating with the Holy Spirit and have miraculous gifts but none comparable to Moses or

Elijah. The worst enemy of faith is doubt and unbelief. Verily, I say unto you, if ye have faith, and doubt not, ye shall not only do this which is done to the fig tree, but also you can move mountains. He that believeth on me, the works that I do shall he do also. The real problem is unbelief, the lack of miracles in any ministry has nothing whatsoever to do with any restrictions of God's promises since we are told that *"all scripture is profitable"*. The Bible puts a strong emphasis on faith. Jesus said to his disciples that if they would trust him they would succeed in the missions before them, It is impossible to please God without faith. God's *word* has the power to bring the fulfillment of its promises. We are thankful for the fact that God's word itself has miracle working power that brings a fulfillment of that which it promises on our behalf. Supernatural gifts are given, not just to the apostles, but to every one of us who are believers. The Bible is full of promises concerning God's willingness to give us miraculous intervention. Our Bible also tells us God does not change his mind to give us miraculous intervention, and furthermore teaching us that God does not change his mind concerning his promises. God said about himself, *"For I am the Lord, I change not."* He does not change his mind to whom he gives his grace. In the last days all his people are promised miraculous power, *"Ye shall become baptized with the Holy Ghost."* God said he would pour out his spirit upon all flesh and they shall prophesy. God made it very clear the supernatural ability to prophesy was not limited to just the apostles nor to a certain age. Miracles are a part of God's covenant promises. The New Testament provides much proof that powers are available to all of God's people who believe. Ordinary Christians can receive gifts by the Holy Spirit.

Part Six

Jesus

Jesus Christ born in Bethlehem of Judea, the Holy babe of Bethlehem. Chosen and ordained by his Father in Heaven to be the Savior of the mortal world and so he became this world's redeemer. His earthly life covered a period of thirty-three years. He was a unique man of distinguishing character who surpassed any greatness our world would ever witness and his mortal existence would become our world's greatest treasure. Jesus stands first and foremost the greatest leader to ever walk on this earth at any time. He was chosen and anointed by God to live with us and then to die for our sins so we could have eternal life. Jesus' public ministry only lasted three years. He preached from the heart with divine authority about his Father's kingdom in Heaven. His immaculate life on earth in the flesh was spotless and without sin. His fame and wondrous life became even greater after his death, after having been denied by his own people, which brought about his violent though voluntary death. All Jesus wanted was to carry out the will of his Father. Because Jesus was born of a mortal mother, he inherited the capacity to die and Jesus voluntarily surrendered his life for our earthly sins. Even though we know he didn't perhaps want to, as he prayed to his Father to take the cup from him, he still voluntarily suffered, and bled, and died. We know he could have stopped the process at any time, but he did not, ergo he voluntarily gave his life for ours. God's plan for his only begotten Son was to die and conquer death and become our worldly redeemer on behalf of all mankind. Jesus' victory over death was made manifest in the resurrection of the crucified Christ. Even as Jesus Christ had his earthly purpose, so has God given every mortal person born to this earth a valuable purpose. John the Baptist said it best when he first noticed Jesus walking up to him on the banks of the Jordan River. John shouted, *"Behold, here comes the one I have been telling you about"* - *"the true sacrificial lamb of God."* Jesus' cousin John was the first to call Jesus the sacrificial lamb. The moment John the Baptist watched Jesus walking toward him, he realized he had fulfilled his own purpose on this earth. Even at a young age John realized it was his purpose to clear a path and prepare people for Jesus' arrival. He announced, *"Here comes the one I have told you about, the one greater than I."* When Jesus died on the cross he fulfilled his father's purpose for him on this earth. Jesus understood this and freely chose, volunteered to die for the salvation of mankind's sins. Jesus not only died for our sins, he died *because* we are sinners. We all are sinners, as even today we continue to sin and we must realize that as such, we are not blameless for Jesus' death. We are all guilty and responsible for Jesus being crucified on the cross. Herod and Pilate only wanted to chastise Jesus and then turn him loose because they felt he was not guilty of any truly serious crimes, certainly nothing that would cause him to be put to death. But the Jewish High Priests, so scared of losing their power, loudly cried out, *"crucify him!"* They, along with an angry mob demanded Jesus' death. These people didn't want anyone interfering with their wicked lifestyles or taking away their power. Is it today, the same as when Jesus was crucified? I can only answer yes. Many people today that hold high power will do anything to hang on to it, no matter the cost, legal or not. The behavior of some of our government officials is a tragedy, it seems our government is moving away from God, having exiled the Bible's teachings from our nation's schools and from many of our public places. No longer are our Ten Commandments proudly displayed on courthouse lawns and in our nation's public facilities, even during Christmas time our Holy Nativity is unwelcome to be on display. These holy icons are being removed as the Democrats continue voting for their removal. Actually, the Democrats voted three times at their National Convention to NOT mention God's name. How far have they fallen away from God? How unrighteous and misguided they have become! Only the church and the Bible block their unrighteous and rebellious behavior for a radical, corrupt society. Our only defense is our nation's spiritual leaders and the churches in America. All of us Christians must wake up and fight for our faith, and speak loudly against this travesty. We are living in a society with two sets of laws; man's laws which are terribly flawed, and the laws of our God which were given to Moses in the form of The Ten Commandments. Laws made by man are often flawed, but God's laws are always first and foremost completely above all others and remain flawless. We must always put God and God's laws first in every aspect of our lives. Remember that if you break man's laws you go to jail, but if you break God's laws you go to hell. So you decide which laws shall come first in your life. Also remember when you die and find yourself standing outside those pearly gates of Heaven, there won't be any Democrats or Republicans waiting there to greet you. It will be Jesus and his angels opening the gates and inviting you in. Many Bible scholars argue there will be a rapture and others state that if there is, will it be before seven years of tribulation or in the middle of the tribulation or will it occur at the end of these difficult times. Apostle Paul described the rapture in the New Testament as happening before the tribulation. Bible prophecy and scriptures point to the rapture happening shortly before the difficult period of tribulation. One may be at a ball game and suddenly one third of all the seats will become empty and the game on the field is stopped because some of the players and officials will have vanished as fast as in the *twinkling of an eye*. The people who are left in the stadium may look around with shocked expressions on their faces and ask each other what just happened? A few will understand they just witnessed the rapture and were caught unprepared. All believers from all over the world will be called up into the air to meet the Lord and receive their new spiritual bodies free of suffering from pain and the agony of fatal diseases. Their new bodies will be built for all eternity, bodies without limitations. The unbelievers and the lukewarm faithful will be left behind to suffer through seven years of the tribulation period. All will not be lost because many of those left behind will find a renewed faith in God because of what they had just witnessed, the miracle of the rapture right before them as they saw those who vanished and went to be with the Lord. Churches will become very active and pews will be filled with new believers. Ministers will go back to preaching the true word of God. The lukewarm before the rapture will likewise afterward become hungry for the truth. Once again people will put God first in their lives and come to realize that God's laws always come before the laws made by man.

Who Do You Say I Am

Jesus asked his disciples, *"Who do you say 1 am?"* and Peter answered him, *"You are the Christ."* Simon Peter was the first to ever call Jesus, The Christ. Simon Peter was also the first to be led to Jesus when his brother Andrew introduced him to Jesus. The life of Jesus is a mystery without an ending; we crucified him, then we accepted that it was for us that he was crucified in the first place. At the age of thirty years old Jesus left his home in Nazareth and went down to the Jordan River to receive the hand of his cousin, John the Baptist. He who had no sin took his place among sinners. It was right in his Father's eyes that this should be after he was baptized. God spoke to him saying, *"Thou art my beloved son."* The gospel records show how Jesus came into conflict with his own people in his ministry. We may even ask ourselves, *"who is this Jesus?"* Well, the apostle Paul spoke of Jesus in this way, stating Jesus' qualities manifested themselves as love, joy, patience, kindness, goodness, faithfulness, gentleness, and self-control. He had all the various virtues and qualities of the good fruits of God. The Gospels identified six groups or classes of people in Jesus' time; the Romans, the Sadducees, the Scribes, the Pharisees, the Herodians, and the Zealots. Now the Romans held the most power as they were the guardians of law and order. It was a time of much hate and prejudice among the various groups of people. (Sounds rather familiar, does it not?) Once a demon-possessed man shouted out to Jesus, *"I know who you are, The Holy One Of God!"* Even an evil spirit could recognize the Son of God, but not the spiritually blinded Pharisees! Jesus never said to anyone who he was, not to anyone. When Peter called Jesus "the Christ", Jesus' heart welled up with joy and he answered Peter with a loving heart. *"Blessed are you Simon, son of Barjona!"* For flesh and blood has not revealed this to you, but my Father who is in Heaven. After this incident Jesus only spoke to his disciples about who he was. And only in the final days when at the end he stood bound before the high priest for judgment and faced the prospect of the cross did he make for the first time the public announcement of his identity. Jesus' ministry was very extraordinary for the time; how dare him to challenge those in authority! He did challenge their authority though, on several occasions; he challenged the high priest by clearing the Temple market, he challenged the authority of the Scribes by setting aside the tradition of the Elders, he challenged the authority of the Pharisees by breaking the Sabbath rule and performing a healing on that day. It is no wonder they all challenged him to state his credentials. They asked Jesus, *"by what authority are you doing these things?"* It is a shame that an evil spirit would know the voice of God, but yet those self-righteous people of power were completely clueless. Jesus' enemies tried but failed in drawing the crowds away from him. They became impressed by the miracles he performed, but they also became frightened of losing their power to a miracle worker. When Jesus Christ makes his place and time of appointment with men, he does not always give his name. Jesus tells us he determines the form and occasion of his presence and where and to whom he will come. Jesus came to us as a suffering servant. The Jews could not (and do not) accept the Son Of God in that kind of form. Jesus promises *"I am with you always and everywhere, and I shall be with you to the end."* Wisemen seeking Jesus traveled from afar guided on the journey by a beauteous star. But if we desire him, he is close at hand. The first disciples asked Jesus, *"where are you staying?"* He said unto them, *"Come and see."* Whereby they went and saw, and what they saw was the Father. Because it was with him that Jesus stayed. So follow the Great I AM who says, *"I am the Bread of Life; I am the Light of the World; I am the Door of the Sheep; I am the Good Shepherd."*

Jesus Preaching

Jesus stirred up masses of people when he preached in Galilee that *"the kingdom of God is at hand, and His kingdom ruleth over all. The son of man is coming on the clouds of Heaven, as unexpected as a thief in the night."* Jesus urged all men to prepare for the coming of Christ to enter the kingdom. Psalm 103: 19 *"The Lord has established His throne in the heavens and His kingdom ruleth over all."* Jesus did not flinch as he preached like the ancient prophets before him, preaching righteousness like the portrayal of God's character. He told crowds their obligations to God was more important than their duty to Caesar or any other earlier, earthly power (this holds true for us today.) Jesus clearly taught that his Father's divine love was like a good shepherd seeking his lost sheep, which defines the loving character of God, our Father. He shared of God's willingness to forgive and be merciful to sinners. Crowds gladly listened to him and hailed him as a prophet. Before Jesus, society had always tended to neglect the outcasts, but Jesus' message was to have love for every person regardless of the burdens they carried. Every individual has a unique and personal value in the eyes of God. Jesus realized fully the overwhelming majesty and holiness of God, and that His nature is never lost from Jesus' thoughts, *"my Father is greater than I"*. Collectively, society has tended to neglect the outcasts of the world, yet Jesus preached his father's divine love for all and God's willingness to forgive all repentant sinners. At one point a publican cried out to God, *"God, be merciful to me, a sinner!"* Jesus' love extended even to those who opposed his teachings and refused his fellowship. Jesus taught his listeners to love their enemies and pray for they that persecuted them; and to be merciful to those who are unjust to us, and to always pray for them. Jesus told his disciples to *"know them by their fruits, each tree is known for its fruits."* Matthew 7:16 Jesus continually taught his disciples the good life is one of constant growth and progress. Never become satisfied or content, always grow and be righteous. There were times when apostle Paul felt unworthy of God's love and wrote in his letters saying he was unworthy to be called an apostle. Near the end of his life he wrote, *"I am less than the least of all of the saints."* I feel none had a fuller understanding of God's words than Paul did, and even Paul, in moments of doubt, held his course and served God loyally to the very end of his days. Paul wrote from prison that he must forget the things behind him and stretch forward to the things which were before him, *"I press on toward the goal"*. Paul never forgot the day God transformed his life on the road to Damascus and he worked hard to repay his debt to God. Paul became a very extraordinary apostle and saint. He understood the riches and graciousness of Jesus Christ. As Jesus preached he also taught love toward God and man. At times, Jesus' vision and his ideals seemed so far above those listening to his sermons, as when he spoke for us not to have lust or anger for others in our hearts and that we should neither kill nor commit adultery. Jesus demanded good will and strong love for all humanity, that if we have Christian love in our hearts this will become our moral guide, teaching that his Father gave us the Ten Commandments to become our highest moral code. It is our duty to use these commandments as our moral compass to guide us through life and practice the laws God gave us. Jesus' teaching

Jesus Preaching

emphasized the importance of forgiveness because he saw it as God's dealings with man. One of the strongest characteristics of a good Christian is their willingness to forgive. Jesus said that no Christian in any circumstances should become vindictive and seek retaliation and revenge, Jesus preached against hatred, and commanded love and forgiveness. Jesus believed the best way to overcome evil is by acts of goodness. Jesus said we will never destroy evil and hatred by responding with revenge. Prevention is better than cure, it is good to help a slave, but better to abolish slavery. Jesus admired the humble spirit. *"Blessed are the poor in spirit"*, a humble spirit is a basic quality of Christian life, Jesus insisted on humility and love as a fundamental principle, as the most noble characters recognize their own poverty.

Jesus Teaching

Jesus called out to the disciples to leave their nets and come to a different kind of catching. He called his handful of followers to launch destruction against the powers of evil. Jesus warned his twelve followers of the great personal risks and the changes they would face following him, as his call demanded the elimination of evil in the world. Jesus bitterly denounced the hypocritical selfishness of the Pharisees, men who claimed to be religious leaders. Jesus preached that honesty in life was a virtue, but the Pharisee-character was a pretense of goodness with very little virtue. Jesus spoke of the hypocrites in the synagogues, saying they had no love of mankind in their hearts; likewise, they had no sympathy for the needy and the helpless, their hearts were cold from selfish power, and there was no compassion in their uncharitable hearts. Jesus preached much about the blessings of heaven which were ready for men, and urged all to enter into it. He said the kingdom is like a treasure hidden in a field. It's like a pearl of great value, worth more than all else that the merchant possesses. Jesus often spoke about good deeds, blessed are the pure in heart; for they shall see God and enter into the kingdom of heaven. Even good deeds done in secret will not be overlooked, preaching that all good acts must be honest acts of sincere love to serve others. *"If I bestow all my goodness to feed the poor...but have not love, it profiteth me nothing."* God knows our hearts. God sees us as we really are, one cannot lie to God. Jesus made it clear in the Sermon On

The Mount to those listening, good acts are not for the approval of man, but of God, *"who sees in secret"*. Jesus taught all good acts of love are always seen by God and remembered, acts done by devotion and love rather than a desire to earn a reward. Jesus made it fully clear in his ministry that his followers should drop their fishing nets, leave their tax booths, and accept his leadership and example. Jesus did not hesitate to demand loyalty to himself and often spoke in the manner of his cousin, John the Baptist who came before him. Whosoever shall lose his life for my sake and the gospel's, shall find it in God's kingdom. The Christian world has always turned to Jesus for its' knowledge of God. Jesus preached his father's love with authority that never wavered and knew his most important task was to reveal God to the world. So long as love leads our lives, so long will Jesus be the leader of our souls.

Jesus Man Of Myth

Some people feel Jesus of Nazareth never lived - that he was only a mythical figure, a spectacular allegory. The Gospels give us a perfectly clear picture of his individual characteristics that are so lively and unmistakable. He stands out so distinctly as himself and not anyone else. Yes, Jesus was real. and yes, he walked this earth, dealing with real people in an actual historical situation of epic proportions. Jesus came to us from a young virgin mother, and was born to unemployed and homeless parents. Common sense should tell us that this is not the way a myth is made and likewise, this is not the way mythical gods are made. Jesus was labeled a Heretic by his own people and a traitor by his government, angering the Pharisees when he called them out and questioned their faith. And they in turn saw him as a fake and an outcast who was a threat to their power. The Jewish high priests thought Jesus a Heretic, claiming Messiahship, who misled the people. And the Christian movement, which was spreading across the region was splitting synagogues and making converts of a false Messiah thereby inviting persecution of the Romans who might confuse Christians with Jews, and in every way hurting and troubling the region. In Paul's early documents and letters he wrote of the very evident, arising conflict between Jews and Christians. Jesus was a "wiseman", a "doer of wonderful works", and the high priests cried that he must die, for he has practiced magic! Jesus' life, ministry and death are unquestioned facts. The historical reliability of the biblical records and gospel narratives must be taken seriously, that Jesus was a real person who lived and taught for much of his thirty-three years and then died on Calvary's Cross. Saul, a hostile persecutor of Christians, was a new born again man (Paul) after his conversion. He was said to be a Pharisee converted to a convinced faith that the Messiah at last had come. So then as Paul, he became close to the disciples and learned the life of Jesus. The true quality of Paul's letters reveal important facts about Jesus' life. Paul himself was labeled a traitor and because of his knowledge of Jesus would also have to die. Perhaps Paul never saw Jesus or listened to him preach, but shortly after the crucifixion Saul the Persecutor became Paul, a devoted follower of Christ and the founder of many churches. His transformation on the road to Damascus was convincing evidence of the true power of God, and further provenance of the life of Jesus. Paul became close friends with the disciples and often traveled with them on ministry missions. They in turn educated Paul with amazing stories of Jesus and his ministry. Paul said, *"It is no longer I who live but Christ who lives in me."* Paul knew Jesus was not a mythical figure. The Gospels are genuine historical documents which provide factual evidence of the real personality and the human qualities of Jesus' life and times. It is deeply disturbing to Christians when anyone calls Jesus a myth. Unfortunately, there will always be enemies of the church who choose to slander and refute authentic records. Our four gospels were written between AD 65 and AD 100, and their authors did the best they could, but despite the authentic, memorable accounts and oral stories and the many written records containing the historic events of Jesus' remarkable life, there were naysayers then and there are naysayers still today. But nothing these naysayers purport can negate what our wonderful Savior accomplished for all of mankind, and it is of note that near the end of Jesus' ministry he was followed by masses of people. Crowds were very large as people gathered to at least catch a glimpse of him, following him and shouting, *"Hosanna to the Son of David!" "Blessed be he who comes in the name of the Lord!" "Hosanna in the highest!"* In the marketplaces some came and laid their invalids in Jesus' path, begging him to heal their loved ones. Others reached out to touch him or even just tried to touch the tassel of his robe or the hem of the garment. Thousands of people witnessed the love of Jesus. Over two thousand years later, he is still followed by masses of people. Jesus is no myth. He lives!

Doubts and Disciples

The confused, scared disciples except for Thomas, gathered in the upper room behind closed doors. They talked among themselves excitedly, being anxious about their future without their Messiah. For three years these loyal men walked with Jesus and learned to boldly spread the news that Jesus told them, that of eternal life. Everywhere they went they became witnesses to great miracles Jesus performed before them. Their powerful leader always provided their every need. At the time, it seemed all hope was lost, as uncertainty gave way to doubt and their faith was beginning to weaken. Suddenly Jesus appeared before the disciples and they were filled with joy and wonder. Jesus reminded them he had already told them about his father's plan, that he must die and rise again, just as the prophets wrote. Jesus explained that he had to suffer on the cross and rise so that every sinner would be able to receive forgiveness and ultimately eternal life. He told his followers he would leave them but would be coming back soon. He calmed their troubled minds and hearts by telling them this: "Peace Be With You". Eight days later the disciples met again, this time behind locked doors for fear of being arrested. The other disciples tried to convince Thomas that Jesus had appeared before them but he refused to believe them. Then Jesus reappeared and suddenly Thomas noticed Jesus as he stood right before him telling Thomas to place his finger inside his body where the spear had run through his side. So Thomas did this and then cried out, *"My Lord, My God, I believe!"*

Doubt is certainly a great enemy to faith, but it is not a sin to doubt. Because of things we do not understand and are unsure of, as humans it is our nature to be doubtful of that which we cannot readily explain, but we must not let doubt weaken our faith as it did Thomas'. We should, we must, remember always that *faith conquers doubt!* Replace doubt with prayer, choose to be a believer, not a doubter. You cannot grow stronger spiritually in doubt - you can only become more confused, but the more your spirit grows in right believing, the stronger your faith will become. You will become a much stronger Christian.

Jesus appeared several more times in the 40 days he remained on earth after his rising from the tomb. He appeared to a crowd of 500 people and preached his father's love for them. He told the people he would return to his father because he was sent to fulfill God's amazing plan to save his children. Telling them he had been spit upon, beaten, and crowned with cruel thorns stuck into his scalp. And then displayed with that crude crown on his head, he was mocked and scorned by wicked sinners. Jesus prayed on the cross for those who crucified him, even while in excruciating pain himself, still he cried out on their behalf, *"forgive them father, for they know not what they do"* - 1 Romans 12:14 And, *"Bless those who persecute you, bless and do not curse"* - Luke 6:36 Jesus, in mortal agony, mercifully forgave from the cross. *Be merciful, just as your father also is merciful.* Jesus told each of his disciples, *I chose you, you did not choose me, remember you are my friends and I have chosen you for a special purpose to go into the world.* Remember I asked you to follow me, I will make you fishers of men. (The following paragraphs are Jesus' words but I have paraphrased some of it and so it does not appear in quotes even though they are Jesus'

Doubt and Disciples

words and directives to his disciples.) You will go out and produce a great harvest of souls. I will command you. But first I have to teach you everything the father has taught me. I have no special favorites, I love all those who obey me and do my father's work. Jesus told his disciples that he loved them the same way his father loved him and his love for each of them was an overflowing love. Jesus told them they must trust him to take care of them, to have peace in their hearts knowing he is always with them [us]. Then, precious ones, go out into the world and reap a great harvest that will live forever, and when you find fruit that is damaged lay hands upon it and make it anew in Christ, don't just pick the best fruit from the tree, though, for all fruit is precious in God's eyes. Much trouble will lay ahead, so hold tight and know I will take care of you, even in the darkest of times, trust me.

"Yes, ask anything using my name, and I will do it." - John 14: 14

"My sheep hear my voice, and I know them, and they follow me." - John 10:27

So Who Is The Holy Spirit

Apostle Paul said the Holy Spirit is the sole (and to my way of thinking, the soul) doctrine of the Christian church. The Holy Spirit is the bestower of power, of joy, and of moral purity. And by its' fruit shall it be known. God promised mankind, "I will pour out my spirit upon all flesh" and that he would give a new heart when placing his spirit within us, and we will receive the breath of the Holy Spirit. At Jesus' baptism by John the Baptist, the Holy Spirit descended upon him. Shortly afterward, Jesus went forth into the wilderness to wrestle with temptations from the devil. The Holy Spirit was within Jesus, and thus he had the power to defeat Satan. *"Baptize in the name of the Father, and of the Son, and of the Holy Spirit."* Matthew 28:19

The spirit is a gift of Christ to his people, those within the Christian fellowship. Scripture recognizes the Holy Spirit as the guiding principle and authority of Christian faith. It should solely become the centerstage of our lives, becoming our divine nature and most significantly for our behavior. The Spirit has a guiding impact upon the souls of all mankind. Throughout the Old Testament the "Spirit" is mentioned no fewer than 378 times. In the New Testament it is mentioned 335 times, and the activity of the Holy Spirit recorded in the Bible is huge and should always be recognized in today's church. The Lord God *"breathed into man's nostrils the breath of life, and man became a living soul"*.

I fear today's modem age church has a meager understanding of the Holy Spirit. We must never neglect our traditional doctrine for the Holy Spirit, for a church without the Spirit will lack in fulfillment. I understand some find the Holy Spirit mystifying and they may struggle to grasp the supernatural power of God. We humans tend toward skepticism when faced with unknowns or that which is perceived as "abnormal". It is in our psyche to want to live "in the natural world", because then we can better explain that which we do not understand. The Holy Spirit is God-at-work within us. Whenever you feel the power of the Holy Spirit you will also feel his living presence, his divine spirit of truth, and you will be shaken and stirred. All strong Christians believe and recognize the powers and mysterious forces of the Spirit. The awareness of the Spirit is a religious awakening. When we receive the Holy Spirit, we receive the Body of Christ within our hearts and souls. We will feel the power of Christ and feel his presence and know his purification and empowerment and better understand the works of God in our lives, knowing without a doubt that God is always near. Apostle Paul had an honest and noble insight of the Holy Spirit, *"The Lord is Spirit"*, for the Spirit which is the Holy Spirit which is the Spirit of God is the Spirit of Christ. Jesus of Nazareth was both fully divine and truly human. Jesus came to us to protect human life. Jesus was made of flesh and spirit and dwelt among us full of love and grace for all. Our Father's greatest gift is clearly his begotten Son, Jesus Christ of Nazareth.

Holy Spirit

Jesus said John the Baptist was the greatest prophet that ever walked the face of the earth. Jesus testified that John the Baptist was over and above Moses, Elijah, and Elisha. What John did for Jesus was no small nor easily obtainable feat, John's assignment was to make a clear path for the arrival of Christ. He embraced this mission with a true heart and carried out this divine accomplishment as he anticipated the arrival of the true Lamb sent by God to die for the sins of the world. Everything God does is prearranged, planned beforehand, God has predestined a plan for all our lives. Some will become anointed with a supernatural ability to accomplish powerful works in the Lord's name. Jesus said the Holy Spirit will bring understanding that will dwell within us. Scriptures tell us with the indwelling presence of the Holy Spirit is God Almighty, resident within us allowing an increased capacity to understand the truth and receive supernatural power for performing miracles. Jesus said those believers who are filled with the Holy Spirit carry within them the one that carries "the anointing", the one that carries the Power of God. Jesus said, *"for He will be with you and will dwell in you. You will know His wisdom and power and do great works in His name."* Knowledge is key to a good life, the more we know and understand the ways of God, the more knowledge we have of God, the more I (we) should realize what an honorable privilege it is to love and serve Almighty God. It is impossible to please God *without faith*. Jesus' disciples marveled at the powerful reality of his words, as Jesus cursed the fig tree and it withered at the roots at the word of Jesus before them. When Jesus cursed the fig tree he activated and released the Holy Spirit with his powerful words. Jesus' faith was so potent it withered the tree as he spoke to it before their eyes. Jesus served and pleased his Father; *"and he who sent me is with me. The Father hath not left me alone; for I do always those things that please him."* John 8:29 God anointed his only son Jesus with the Holy Spirit and sent him with the necessary power to heal and to do good works in His name. Most importantly, Jesus came to destroy the evil works of the devil. Jesus knew his father was always with him at all times, in difficult times as well as in more peaceful times, because the Holy Spirit dwelt within him. He was sent to us with a specific assignment empowered by the Holy Spirit to defeat and destroy the works of the devil, and to deliver the promise of salvation. When God anoints, it is a conferment and divine assignment, and the recipients of such will receive the Holy Spirit with all the ability, authority, and power to operate and carry out their assignments, *"for God will be with you"*. Jesus often sent his disciples out in pairs to fulfill assignments, first they prayed and then Jesus put the Holy Spirit in them, telling them not to take anything with them so they would learn to depend on God alone to provide their needs. They were told to fulfill the heavenly Father's ministry with deeds of love and kindness, to heal and help the needy; that every step they would take should make a union and fellowship with Christ, learning and understanding the ways of God, for that was the work of their calling.

I am personally sure that when Jesus sent out his disciples to preach the gospel he made it clear to them they had the best of God's resources and were therefore equipped with every available tool to fulfill their given assignments. But most importantly, they were filled with the power of the Holy Spirit and never alone on their journey. They returned excited, knowing they were better men for understanding the benefit of serving a loving God. Jesus told them to focus on their assignment, and the Lord would guide them and provide for their needs, so they should go out and make the assignment their focus. *"For the kingdom of God is not meat and drink; but righteousness, and peace, and joy in the Holy Ghost."* Romans 14:17.

The disciples went to all villages to teach the people the true power of God, and at every opportunity they laid hands on and healed the sick. With every healing the disciples felt a great fullness of joy that reached out to the Holy Spirit in their hearts. They felt a new level of purpose coupled with a new understanding of how it is indeed more rewarding to give than to receive. They realized also the source of their strength was the joy of spiritual fruit, for the scriptures tell us, *"for the joy of the Lord is your strength."* God Almighty has the ability to change all lives, enabling all of us to have the Holy Spirit dwelling in our hearts. Only from the grace of God can we receive the true treasure of the Holy Spirit in our souls. Scriptures tell us we shall serve and live in God's plan. *"You shall call upon me, and pray to me, I will hear you and you shall seek and search for me with all your heart."* These words are God's plan for a spirit-filled life. This is God's ultimate plan to guide us by his spirit in peace. God today is still working in our everyday lives, providing us with every available resource and benefit his twelve disciples had available to them. We must serve today even as his disciples of the past served. God has thoroughly equipped and furnished us with every possible resource for today's discipleship so that we may continue to serve and to preach the gospel. And every Christian has a divine agenda, which should be to help those who are lost to find their way to the Lord so that they may also seek his promise of eternal life.

Is The Devil Real

Throughout the Bible the Devil and Satan are described as the old serpent that deceived the whole world starting with Adam and Eve in the garden. Satan was a powerful angel cast out of Heaven because he opposed God, attempting to set up his own authority. He abandoned his position with God because he wanted authority and power like God has. The Devil is a gifted spirit with superior intelligence but he falls short of the power of God. Satan is a deceitful, counterfeit king, walking on Earth as a roaring lion looking for lost sheep gone astray. The Devil seduces mankind at its' weakest moment. He is a tirelessly deceitful worker always tempting and coaxing mankind away from God. Please never doubt for a moment the existence of the Devil. He is a real, evil spirit with his own agenda and his own supernatural powers. Adam and Eve paid a huge price for listening to the Devil, and because they listened to the Devil they lost a perfect life in the garden which previously had no sin or death. Adam did not recognize his sin against God until it was too late. But many years later, apostle Paul recognized the dreaded enemy Satan, and cried out, *"O wretched man that I am!"* Adam was made without blemish or sin, as God made Adam in his own image. Adam was granted freedom of choice, (as we are). Eve was granted freedom of choice. (as we are). Adam made his choice. And Eve made her choice. And because of their choice, all humanity suffered the consequences of sin. God warned Adam and Eve not to eat from the Tree of Knowledge and because of their sin, their descendants must continually suffer the penalty of physical death. God made man and his world good but sin spoiled it. No one likes to be told they are sinners, but every person on this earth is a sinner in the eyes of God. God called sin a tragedy, a "human weakness". God tells man that those who reject his word shut the door to Heaven and open the door to Hell when they deny the miracle of Christ. Jesus said, *"For what shall it profit a man, if he gain the whole world, and suffer the loss of his soul?"* and *"the soul that sinneth, it shall die"*. Man's only salvation from sin was the death of the Lamb of God upon the cross. His death and resurrection is our promise of salvation. Jesus died on the cross to break the bonds of sin and damnation.

Seeker Of Truth

Jesus said, *"You shall know the truth, and the truth shall make you free."* Every Christian is a seeker of the truth, but our scientific world also seeks the truth. The most beautiful thing about science is not its' discoveries, scientists seek the truth as Christians do, and many search for that truth with great passion and some seem to have an almost humble willingness to follow all facts to whatever end those facts may lead them to. Unfortunately, throughout the world there are some in the scientific realm that bear anti religious views. The secrets of Heaven and Earth are open to those who seek the truth with straightforward open minds and hearts. Christ is the very essence of the love of truth and reality. The most popular book in the world is our Bible, written thousands of years ago, which is filled with scientific facts. Sadly, people will always debate on the subject of does God exist? Many of our scientists are realizing that prophecy in scriptures written 2,000 plus years ago is becoming reality right before their very eyes. Science is now realizing that the Bible is no ordinary book. It is a book of truth which is full of incredible facts about life and a future life with Christ. I feel the Bible is the history book that not only tells us of our past but also tells us in great detail, our future. I describe the Bible as a key that can unlock incredible mysteries of the world. Scriptures read today point with great accuracy to the conflict in the Middle East. Bible predictions written centuries ago tell us of the rise and fall of great nations. It predicted the rebirth of Israel May 14, 1948, *"Born in one day"*. The Bible warns of increasing earthquakes in various places, and to look for signs in the sun, moon and stars. Ancient scriptures tell us of persecution of followers of the Christian faith in all nations, and warns us of false teachers coming into the churches and leading many followers astray. Undeniable evidence points to the authentic reliability of the Bible. Every day in the Middle East archaeological discoveries tell us the Bible is 100 percent trustworthy. Any skeptics who would declare the Bible to be wrong are blind to the facts and are sadly mistaken, being in a state of gross denial and in my opinion, deniers of the truth. A child may ask, "Is God as good as Jesus?" But the real question is, is Jesus as good as God? The obvious answer is a resounding yes, Jesus and the Father are one, with Jesus being the human life of God, something hard for some of us to grasp at times. Jesus came to us as truly human, living on earth as a man. Yes, he did perform miracles, but only for others and in answer to human need. He performed no miracles for himself. He could have saved himself but chose instead to die for our sins. Jesus spoke to crowds in the villages using his father's words. In a sense, Jesus was God's mediator who expressed his love for all. My devotion to God is not one of duty, but one of privilege, I am privileged to serve a risen Savior. One of today's greatest prerogatives in Christian life is to become a disciple, showing others in society our Christian humanity in speech and attitude with a willingness to serve others' needs. Jesus taught devotion and love rather than a desire to earn a reward. Oftentimes scientists speak of the universe in five-part terminology; Time, Space, Matter, Power, and Motion. In Genesis 1: 1-5, God tells us he controls ALL aspects of the universe he created. He is the creator of all things that exist. Amen. I place an Amen on it because even in such profundity, sometimes one simply must put an Amen on it. So again I say, Amen.

Jesus And Woman

Women were first at the cradle and last at the cross. Let that sink in for a moment. A woman in a crowd shouted to Jesus, *"Blessed is the womb that bore you, and the breast that you sucked!"* Jesus spoke back to the woman telling her, *"Blessed rather are those who hear the word of God and Keep it!"* Men held all the legal power in those primitive times and divorce was very ugly because men were always judge, jury and sometimes executioner. One day Jesus came to the defense of a woman accused of adultery who was surrounded by angry men ready to stone her to death. Jesus turned on the group of men telling them to let him who is without sin among them to be the first to throw a stone at her. He spoke further saying, there is the double standard for men and women in the morality of sex. Jesus was denying these men's right to lord it over women by the Mosaic law. The men ashamedly dropped their heads and slowly walked away. Then Jesus spoke to the accused woman, *"neither do I condemn you. Go, and do not sin again."* Jesus tried hard to break down unfair barriers as he understood the Mosaic law was a cruel law for women. The Pharisees could not understand why Jesus preached against and protested for better treatment of women. John's Gospel tells us of Jesus meeting a woman of Samaria at a well. This particular woman had had five husbands and was now living with a man not her husband. When Jesus' disciples walked up and saw him [Jesus] talking to the woman at the well, they marveled that he was talking to a stranger and a Samaritan woman at that, (those who were looked down upon by the Jews whether male or female), they were at best puzzled and at worst shocked. But Jesus broke down all the ancient barriers for which he had little or no regard. On another day a woman with a serious bleeding problem pushed her way through a crowd and reached out and touched the hem of his garment. Jesus suddenly stopped, remarking that someone who was in pain had touched him. *"Please step forward,"* he said. The timid woman stepped forward and stood before Jesus and told him her problem. This act is proof that not only does Jesus know our pain, but he also *feels* our pain. While visiting the home of Martha and Mary, Martha became upset because she was doing all the work preparing the evening meal as her sister sat at Jesus' feet listening to his words. Martha complained to Jesus that it was unfair and that her sister should come help in the kitchen. Jesus lovingly explained to Martha that there are many ways to serve Christ, that she served him by preparing a meal and Mary served him by hearing about His Father. Mark's records confirm the love displayed by the women followers of Jesus. At the crucifixion Jesus' closest friend and loyal follower, Mary Magdalene, and Mary, the mother of James the younger, and of Joses and Salome, who, when he was in Galilee, followed him and ministered to him, along with many other women who came to Jerusalem. Jesus spoke to the women as he went up to Calvary saying, *"Daughters of Jerusalem, do not weep for me, but weep for yourselves, and for your children"*. Jesus had a special relationship with women and they had never before known a man like him. Indeed, the first man to ever understand their needs.

Jesus And Children

Luke spoke of Jesus and children. At first the disciples saw children as a disturbing nuisance and tried to brush them aside as they often asked for bread and fish. Jesus told his disciples, *"Let the children come unto me; do not hinder them"*, and so oftentimes parents would bring their babes to Jesus to receive his blessings. Everywhere he went, he caused a great stir, his fame spread throughout the region. Huge crowds gathered around him, with people trying to touch him or his robe and the disciples were always in close proximity protecting him and shielding him from harm. The *one* John the Baptist preached so boldly about on the banks of the Jordan River had finally arrived; the *one* John spoke about that is greater than he. The consequence of Jesus' popularity would eventually cost him his life, as Jesus' fame became his most dangerous problem. Often when children would see Jesus in the temple they loudly shouted, *"Hosanna!"* Their loud shouting angered the priests who protested this kind of behavior. But Jesus loved them and spoke, *"out of the mouths of babes and sucklings thou hast brought perfect praise"*. Jesus had fond memories of his own childhood, having grown up in a large, loving family surrounded by younger brothers and sisters. Jesus' love and understanding for children was evident, he was happiest when children were near. One day Jesus noticed the disciples arguing among themselves as to who was the greatest. Jesus placed a small child before them, saying, *"whoever humbles himself like this child, he is the greatest in the kingdom of Heaven"*. Jesus identified himself with children when he said, *"to welcome one such child is to welcome me"*. Jesus' personal affection for children was a unique and beautiful thing. And every child adored his gentle ways and loved being in his presence. Jesus was very sympathetic toward the care for women and children in those ancient times. Jesus spoke to women when he preached, and he was painfully aware of the injustices women and children suffered. He said, *"he who robs widows and orphans is as though he robbed God himself"*.

Science says that we need at least four basic elements to survive.

1. Water
2. Air
3. Food
4. Light

And Look what the Bible tells us about Jesus Christ

1. I am the Living Water
2. I am the Breath of Life
3. I am the Bread of Life
4. I am the Light of the World

Science was right, WE NEED JESUS TO LIVE!

Part Seven

Jesus And Enemies

Herod had tried to kill the child Jesus, even as he had killed the children of Bethlehem, but Jesus' family fled to Egypt. Jesus recognized his father's love for Israel and Israel played a tremendous role in Jesus' life. He fulfilled his father's wishes and the destiny of Israel. There is little doubt about Jesus' love for Israel. When Jesus was crucified, his cross bore the inscription, *"Jesus of Nazareth, King of the Jews."* Remember, we crucified him. Then we accepted that it was for us that he was crucified. Israel was both instrumental in and witness to Jesus' love and public ministry. At the age of thirty, he left his home in Nazareth and went to the river Jordan to receive, at the hands of John the Baptist, the baptism of repentance for the remission of sins. He who had no sin took his place among sinners. Jesus would later challenge the authority of the high priest and the Jewish church by clearing the Temple market. He broke the Sabbath rule by healing on the Sabbath, he ate with publicans and sinners, he befriended a woman who was caught in adultery, and that same woman anointed his feet with oil. Some found Jesus' ministry completely confusing. They announced Jesus' authority and power was the works of the Devil. They called him a low born, uneducated imposter. He was only a carpenter's son, how could this simple man and son of a carpenter claim to be the Son of God! Jesus left his enemies and went into the hills and prayed, asking his heavenly father for guidance. When Jesus returned to his disciples, they noticed his teaching style had changed. Jesus now began speaking largely in the form of parables and his ministry became more urgent and active. Jesus explained to his disciples the purpose of speaking in parables, telling them he was speaking in the form in which faith alone can grasp, as well as in a way the hearers would not easily forget so that the lessons remained in their memory, available for the apprehension of faith. The crowds saw in Jesus a breadth of power of love which was not easy to deny. Jesus' family and his disciples became greatly concerned for his safety and well-being, knowing he was overworked and needed rest. Mary and Jesus' brothers went looking for him and found him in the midst of a crowd and sent for him. Jesus refused to come to them, but he sent a significant reply, *"who is my mother and who are my brothers?"* He pointed to his disciples and said, *"here are my mother and brothers!"* for whoever does the will of my Father in Heaven is my brother, and sister, and mother. Then after this Jesus' life drew more swiftly closer to the cross. One of Jesus' main concerns and that which occupied much of his time, was preparing and training his disciples for the decisive struggles that lay ahead of them. Jesus spent almost all of this period of time in training, and his preaching was for the disciples as well as the curious crowds. He was oftentimes tired and would lie down in the boat and fall asleep. On this one certain occasion Jesus was particularly tired of body and soul and was resting as the disciples rowed him across the lake toward Galilee. Jairus, one of the rulers of the synagogue ask for Jesus to come and heal his sick daughter, but she died before Jesus could come to her. Jesus went to her anyway, and he raised her from the dead. This amazing event was witnessed by Peter, James, and John, and it was a turning point in their faith. Then Jesus went to his hometown of Nazareth to visit and say goodbye. Sadly, his townsmen became so upset by his teachings that they threatened to kill him by throwing him down a steep hill. Jesus, perceiving their intentions, turned around and faced them and they fell back, allowing Jesus to leave unharmed. Jesus expressed his sorrow to his disciples, that his own hometown people not only rejected him, but they wanted to kill him. Jesus turned his back from Nazareth and said goodbye forever knowing the end was nearing. Jesus' enemies planned and plotted different ways of getting rid of him, they discussed waylaying him on the road, and many other schemes to rid themselves of this rebel. After Jesus received the sad news of his cousin and faithful servant, John the Baptist's beheading, it was as though the skies darkened over them even as a shadow of the cross and the events yet to unfold. Jesus spoke to his disciples about the hardships and suffering that was to come upon him, telling them to be brave for they, too, must be prepared to face persecution.

Luke 14:27 *"Whoever does not bear his own cross and come after me,"* he said, *"cannot be my disciple."* Jesus was aware there were those who planned to bear false witness against him if he was ever brought to trial. It was essential for Jesus' enemies that he be destroyed. Jesus saw no way out of their difficulties, so he prepared for the final conflict by sending out his disciples on a mission of their own. The disciples returned from their mission with stories of great success and Jesus was proud and gave them much praise. Soon after the return of the disciples a great crowd gathered around Jesus and he taught them. That evening, Jesus told his disciples to feed the huge crowd with only a few loaves and fishes brought by a young lad. The crowd became wild with excitement because of what Jesus had done feeding them with such a few loaves and fishes. Indeed, they had witnessed a miracle, even the disciples were excited, doubly so, since they had just returned from such a successful mission. The crowd surged around Jesus and asked him to be their king. He refused the crown and sent the crowd away. Jesus needed a break to prepare for the final conflict. And at this time Jesus' teaching took on an almost tangible quality and a much deeper urgency. He told all curious followers to please go away as he needed conference time only with his faithful disciples. He asked his disciples, *"Will you also go away?"* Simon Peter replied for them all when he said, *"Lord, to whom shall we go? Thou hast the words of eternal life."* - John 6:67-68

Jesus rallied his disciples and took them quietly away to far-off Phoenicia. There he was unknown and could spend the necessary alone time with his faithful disciples. He wanted to spend unhurried time with them, away from danger and the many enemies wanting to destroy them. Jesus understood it was a calm before the storm. The disciples gathered around their teacher and he taught them about the difficulties to come. It was a happy break, but each disciple could not help their fear for the future events that would yet come to pass. All their fears and concerns would soon become stark reality.

Enemy Of God

Anti-God crusader Madalyn Murray O'Hair waged war on God and religion in the early 1960's, taking her battle all the way to the United States Supreme Court. That godless woman succeeded in having the Bible (and the reading of the Bible), as well as the recitation of prayer banned from American public schools. Today, because of this radical, foul-mouthed woman, who hated God and Christians, any reference to God and the Bible is strictly forbidden in our schools. O'Hair chose our public schools for her battlefield and her chief enemy was God. She was responsible for expelling God from our schools. During this time period, O'Hair shocked and angered millions of television viewers by tearing up a Bible on the Phil Donahue Show. I find it extremely odd that someone would fight so hard against something she did not believe in. She was a member of both the Socialist Labor Party and the Socialist Workers Party, and also found support with some radical, leftist liberals of that time period. O'Hair felt that Christians were brainless, stupid fools, and she loved portraying herself the victim in her cause as she had clearly earned the title, *the most hated woman in America*. To me, and to countless others, her only achievement was hate. Alas, Madalyn Murray O'Hair's life was on a violent collision course with death and so it happened in 1995 that she, her son, Jon and her granddaughter, Robin were kidnapped and tortured before being killed. I'm sure Ms. O'Hair knew that she was about to die and I cannot help but wonder if in those last hours before her death, did she break down and ask God for forgiveness? I hope she did. What a sad life!

Repent From Sin

Jesus said there is only one way back to God, except ye be converted and become as little children. Jesus demands a total conversion, or we shall not enter the Kingdom of Heaven. God cannot tolerate sin because sin separates us from his grace. What is conversion? Conversion means to turn around, or to change direction. And to experience religion and receive grace and gain assurance and to change one's mindset. Conversion can be an instantaneous event, a person can receive a revelation of God's love in a split second and cross a line between darkness and light, between death and everlasting life. It is a huge turning point. It is a conscious acceptance of Christ as one's personal Savior and the yielding of one's life away from sin. A spiritual acceptance of the Bible conversion is a supernatural experience. John described in Jesus' early ministry that hundreds of people followed Jesus. Jesus would not commit himself to them because he knew the hearts of all men, saying they believe with their heads and not with their hearts. Only a total conversion to Christ can save your soul and change your life. It is a change in your thinking as well as an intellectual acceptance of Christ. When we take this step, Christ will be demanding these changes in our lives. When we accept the Holy Spirit we realize that we are sinners and at that precise moment a miraculous new birth takes place. We actually become a newly moral child of God, wanting to live to please him. When one accepts the Holy Ghost, living the Christian life will be placed above all other concerns and the acceptors will turn away from the bleak, empty world and find peace with God. On the day of Pentecost, Peter preached repentance, his sermon was full of power as he spoke, telling individuals that they must repent their sins and accept Christ by faith. Jesus' first sermon ever preached was *Repent*. Sadly, today's modern church seldom ever mentions sin or repentance as these two words have become very unpopular terms that could upset those sitting in the pews. We are so worried about being politically correct that we have forgotten what it is to be holy and repentant. Jesus spoke about his father's kingdom at hand and repentance is mentioned seventy times in the New Testament. The Bible says God *commands* repentance. To repent also demands actions to turn away from sin and to change ourselves. Paul preached repentance to Jews and Greeks, promising them the Lord Jesus Christ would pour out his love, grace, and mercy upon them and that they would acquire a new attitude and know the grace of God and receive eternal salvation. Some of the most popular people of the Bible knew and understood that they were sinners. Peter spoke of his sins saying, *"I am a sinful man"*, and calling himself the *chief of sinners*. And remember that Job became convinced that he was a sinner and said about himself, *"I abhor myself"*. Isaiah spoke of his sins and said, *"Woe is me! I am a man of unclean lips."* I fear many of today's modern-age churches have lost sight of what the Bible means when it talks about sin and repentance. Just saying you're sorry to God is not enough. God demands immediate change, therefore we must turn away from sin.

Part Eight

Second Coming

Sadly, even tragically, some people feel the second coming of Jesus Christ is only a superstition or view it as a dire doomsday prediction. Many of our modern preachers are afraid to even mention the most important books of the Bible Revelation; these books tell about the destruction of mankind and the preachers don't want to preach God's warning because they find this subject too disturbing. It seems that people today don't want a real good sermon, instead they want a feel good sermon. Many of our modern day preachers are doing just that, preaching what people want to hear and not what they need to hear. I find it very unsettling that some modern preachers are not preaching the true word of God. It is an injustice to all church goers everywhere when ministers fail to preach the second coming of Christ. All of you false teachers should lay down your Bibles and go sell timeshares because all you really are is motivational speakers. If you are scared to preach the entire Bible, the true word of God, then you do not belong behind a pulpit. Some people may find the next pages disturbing and feel I have a pessimistic view of life. However, I rejoice awaiting the second coming of Christ Jesus which is promised. And if you are not looking forward to His coming, you may not be going with Him when he returns to Heaven. We have a choice, we may choose between right or wrong, good or evil. Jesus warns us in scriptures over and over again that he will return. He is not trying to scare us, he is trying to prepare us, to save us from sin in the last days. Today all the world's so-called norms have become broken.

Today's civilization is polluted with sin. To me, it seems we are living in the last generation of mankind, the human race, and with every passing day we are hurtling toward the calamitous events that will unfold the end times. From Genesis to Revelation, the Bible warns us of future events events that await the climax of history, and scripture foretells future events and gives us an adequate picture of God's revelation concerning the future of mankind. You will find within the pages of the Bible the course of humanity and its' future. Holy scripture gives readers an adequate picture of events to come. Jesus promised us a second coming and it will eventually happen. All of us must realize that Jesus' words are true and that he keeps his promises. Jesus will return to claim his bride, and sadly there will be tragedy and destruction to civilization before his arrival. For every time the Bible speaks of the first coming of Christ, there are eight times that give reference to his second coming. There are three hundred and eighteen references to this. Over and over the Bible emphasizes the second return of Jesus Christ. *"For see, the Lord will come with fire and with swift chariots of doom to pour out the fury of his anger and his hot rebuke with flames of fire."* Isaiah 66:15 Ezekiel tells us Jerusalem will be restored and the Temple will be rebuilt shortly before Christ returns. Amos tells us the new throne of David will be established again in Jerusalem. John said Jesus told him, *"I go to prepare a place for you. I will come again and receive you unto myself."* The Bible is a treasure chest of proof promising us the second coming. Paul said of the coming of Christ that it was to awaken and raise the dead. Corinthians describes the new house we shall have when this earthly house has dissolved. Not only is the Old Testament filled with promises of Christ's coming, the New Testament also promises the second coming of Christ. The Bible tells us only the truth, that Jesus will come again and it will be a glorious, thrilling time for all Christians who await the reward of Christ. All Christians should prepare their lives for Christ's return. The exact time and date are unknown, not even the angels in Heaven know the day nor the hour, only God himself is aware of the exact moment. Jesus bids us to watch for signs in the sun and the moon, in the distress of nations upon the earth, in the roaring of waves on our waters, and in men's hearts, which will fail them from fear as the earth shakes. Current events today tell us that Bible scriptures are coming true before our eyes. Are we living in the final days of our earth's life? Daniel kept his prophecies a secret, sealed up so as not to be misunderstood until the end times when he spoke of a vast increase in knowledge and travel. Perhaps Daniel is speaking of space travel and computer technology. Never before in the history of the world have we made such leaps and bounds in knowledge and travel within such a short period of time. In the last days Jesus tells us his kingdom will stretch from shore to shore and everyone in our world will have knowledge of the love of God. It will cover the earth because of all this technology. Then He will come. Zechariah 14 tells us to watch, for the day of the Lord is coming soon! On that day the Lord will gather together the nations to fight Jerusalem; the city will be taken, the houses rifled, the loot divided, the women raped; half the population will be taken away as slaves and the other half will be left in what remains of the city. Jesus will return on the Mount of Olives and when his feet touch down the mountain will split in half. Then the Lord will go out fully armed for war, to fight against those nations that have come to harm Jerusalem. And the Lord will send a plague on all the people who fought Jerusalem. And the Lord shall be king over all the Earth. In that day there shall be one Lord, His name alone will be worshipped. *"Let all who can hear, listen to what the Spirit is saying to the churches."* Revelation 3:6

"Wake up! Strengthen what remains and is about to die, for I have not found your deeds complete in the sight of my God. Remember, therefore, what you have received and heard; obey it, and repent. But if you do not wake up, I will come like a thief, and you will not know at what time I will come to you." Revelation 3:2-3

Land Of Jesus

Israel is the most important nation in our world. It is where it all begins and it will play a vital role when it all ends. To some, Israel is the most beloved nation anywhere, yet for some others it is the most hated nation anywhere, from one extreme to the other. Israel is only a small dot of land on our planet, about the size of New Jersey, in the United States of America. It is a beautiful oasis-flower surrounded by weeds. But in John 15:18 it says, *"If the world hates you, keep in mind that it hated me first."* Israel is a land where ancient history merges with today's modern world; in a most unique way the past and present become woven together. I'm told it is impossible not to feel the presence of Jesus while visiting at all the Holy sites, [even though in our modern day, gazing across the way one may see the McDonald's arches]. Some of today's top technology and software comes from this beautiful land. It is the home of the first cell phone and it is one of a dozen nations that launches its own satellites. It has the highest rate of entrepreneurship in the world. And in regard to populations, Israel has the highest ratio of earned college degrees. It is not only a smart place, it is the most healthy of places in the world to live, with a life expectancy of eighty-two years. And it is the only modern democracy in the Middle East. Israel is also one of the largest exporters of flowers in the world; sending 60 million flowers to Europe alone last Valentine's Day. Today, 160,000 Christians, or two percent of the population, call Israel home. The harsh reality is that all citizens live constantly on high military alert. The

Jewish troops today are the best-trained in the world with the best weaponry, they are a fact-mobilized force. Their tough, brave, resilient soldiers have heard stories from their surviving parents about the death camps of the Holocaust. Their motto is *"Never Again"*. Every healthy young citizen has an obligation to serve in Israel's defense forces. It's *mandatory* for all healthy and service-worthy eighteen year olds to serve in the Israeli militia; females serve for two years, and the males serve for three years. All Jewish troops are divinely inspired to defend their nation and their faith. All Israeli citizens understand the danger they constantly live with, but they are brave and resilient and stay ever on the alert; they do not take for granted nor ignore their surroundings. The Six Day War proved to the world just how well and ably Jewish soldiers can fight. Jewish soldiers shed tears of absolute joy when they regained possession of the western wall, better known at the time as the *Wailing Wall.*

Isaiah 52:1 *"Jerusalem, be strong and great again! Holy City of God, clothe yourself with splendor! The heathen will never enter your gates again."* Isaiah 52: 10 *"The Lord will use his holy power, He will save his people and all the world will see it."*

Isaiah 54: 15 *"If anyone attacks you, he does it without my consent; whoever fights against you will fall."*

Sitting in Ford's Theater, Abraham Lincoln told his wife, *"Now the war is over, I can rest. I would love very much to see Jerusalem."* Shortly after uttering these words, Lincoln was assassinated. No race of people on Earth has suffered such racial hatred and persecution as have the Jewish people. They have become scattered among the nations, and slaughtered like so many sheep.

Hitler exterminated one-third of the world's Jews. Six million Jews were starved, tortured, and subjected to heinous atrocities before being destroyed. Jesus compared the Jewish nation to a fig tree. When the fig tree begins to bud again, end times are near. The fig tree budding is a promising symbol of Christ's return. The returning of the Jews from the four corners of the world to their promised land is a true sign of Jesus' return. God's ancient people are returning and building an empire. This is where God wants His ancient people to be. The return of Christ is at hand, our Bibles are powerful witness for that day which is drawing near. President Donald Trump understands the importance of Israel in the eyes of God. He knows that if we ignore Israel, we also ignore God. Jerusalem is the only capital God has ever given any nation.

Psalm 122:6 *"Pray for the peace of Jerusalem, may they prosper."*

On December 6, 2017 our courageous President Trump announced to the world that he would move the American Embassy to Jerusalem. Other American Presidents also made that same promise, but they failed to keep their promises for lack of courage. A large part of the world became angry with Mr. Trump's decision, but our President proved strong in his leadership and honored his promise. As a result, President Trump is highly praised as a hero in Israel.

Isaiah 60:1 *"Arise Jerusalem, and shine like the sun, the glory of the Lord is shining in Israel."*

Psalm 122:6 *"Pray for the peace of Jerusalem. May all who love this city prosper."*

Death And After

No one likes to talk about death, it is a subject that most people try to dismiss as quickly as possible, especially when it concerns themselves or someone they love. From the very moment we are born our battle with death begins. With every grain of sand falling within the hourglass our date with death moves ever closer, our appointment with the grim reaper, that dreaded image of our demise awaits. Of course, if we are Christians, death is not near so grim. Along with aging comes these certain eventualities, that our vision will fade, our teeth will become fewer and will begin to decay and our skin to sag and wrinkle. As we age, we will realize we have begun to move closer to physical death. No matter how much we struggle and try we will never get out of this world alive. In the end, death will always be the victor. Thank God this is only a temporary state as those of us who believe in God will claim victory over death. The soul reason for Jesus' death. You read that right. I did not mean sole - I meant soul. The Christian faith tells us to enjoy life but also to prepare for death. The Bible tells us that there are actually two deaths; one is our physical death and the other is eternal death. Jesus warned that we are to fear the second death far more than the first death. Jesus described the second death as Hell, eternal separation from God. Jesus tells us that the death of the human body is nothing compared to the everlasting banishment of a soul from God. Jesus conquered death on the cross and took the sting out of death. Jesus urges us to be more concerned with the eternal death of the soul, i.e., to be banished from God for eternity. Heaven is one of the greatest mysteries of the Bible. Some people question if Heaven is a real place, but our Jesus said, *"I go to prepare a place for you,"*...in my Father's house there are many rooms. As a Christian I see death as a renewal, a rebirth to a much better life with my Savior, Jesus Christ in beautiful Heaven. When we receive Jesus as our personal Savior, our eternal souls will live forever. It is my feeling the first thing we will realize in Heaven is that our old broken-down, worn-out earthly bodies will be gone, replaced with new spiritual bodies built for eternity. Bodies that will never know age, sorrow, tragedy, disease, darkness, suffering nor death. We will become mesmerized by the cleanliness of Heaven's air, as it will be much different than our unpleasant and often polluted air here on Earth. Heaven's air will have a sweet freshness for us to enjoy as our eyes will be opened to perfect sight and we will be continually amazed at the extraordinarily beautiful sights that shall surround us. We will realize then we are in a perfect garden full of majestic trees, plants, and flowers of every kind and color just bursting with life. So vibrant will these trees and flowers be that absolute joy will exude from them with life and the fullness of their being which will resonate at a soul deep level. There will be birds of every size and color, colors that defy description because we have yet to experience such beauty. I picture these birds singing in the trees, singing songs of praise and worship, the most beautiful sounds we shall ever hear. All those "things" we worked so hard to acquire on Earth shall have no worth in Heaven. We will live for our love for God and one another. No one will ever judge anyone else by their wealth, their physicality, or their skin. In Heaven everyone is one hundred percent equal, living only to love God and to be loved. Apostle Paul spoke of being blinded by a light and experiencing a vision. Paul learned about the afterlife and kind of body the once dead will have in Heaven, he described the earthly body as weak and ugly but that the new, eternal, spiritual body will be strong and beautiful and of no age. As a Christian, I truly feel that when our physical body dies, our soul leaves it and enters a spiritual body built for eternity. Being a Christian, I think of death as a rebirth into Christ in Heaven. Some people question if Hell is a real place, understandably the subject of Hell is not a very pleasant one to contemplate and there are various schools of thought concerning Hell and what or where it actually is. The Bible teaches that our souls will live forever in one of two places, Heaven or Hell. If you are not a Christian your soul will go immediately to a place Jesus called Hades to await God's judgment. The Bible further teaches that whether we are saved or lost, there is conscious and everlasting existence of the soul and personality. The Bible is continually warning us about sin and the day of judgment. On Earth God offers us many chances to accept Him. After death there will be no "second chances" to accept Christ. When we stand before God and he opens the Book of Life will we be cast into the lake of fire? Good Question. As it is written, "There shall be wailing and gnashing of teeth." They shall drink of the wine of the wrath of God and become tormented with fire and brimstone, lost forever and banished from God because they refused to receive God. Every man who willingly and knowingly rejects Christ as Lord and Savior will become tormented in flames. God does not *send* anyone to Hell. Rather, when man refuses God and His offer of salvation, man condemns himself. Mankind's stupidity and blindness in loving sinful pleasures rather than obedience to God keeps us away from salvation. Four words in the Bible translated means Hell. First is Sheol translated thirty-one times. Second is Hades translated ten times in the New

Testament, third is Tartarus used only once in 2 Peter 2:4, and fourth is Gehenna used eleven times. When the Bible speaks of Hell it figuratively speaks of fire that does not consume but burns for eternity. Will our souls be found in Hell one minute after judgment? We must read our Bibles and analyze our life's problems and find an intellectual understanding of God's plan for our lives. We must choose light and avoid darkness.

Closing

I am aware my book will be criticized by some and applauded by others. And I am sure some will accuse me of having rather negative and pessimistic views, but I like to call such views a reality check. Just because we don't acknowledge a problem doesn't mean it doesn't exist. It just means we are not seeing what is happening around us.

In today's society we seem to be living in an age of high anxiety that never before has been so evident. We constantly are subjected to fear and uncertainty and our political freedoms are under attack and have turned democracy into political hatred and corruption. I fear the sands in America's hourglass are rapidly falling away and nearing the final hour.

We are living in a crucial period in our nation's history where many Americans are placing man's law above those of God, and there is an unwillingness to learn and obey God's laws. Americans are becoming desperately weary of this hatred and greed within our political parties and the general reluctance of many to work together for the good of its citizens. We must recognize that our nation has radically changed in just a few year's time. I pray America will come together and work as a team so as not to become destroyed from within by our own hand.

America's problems are not hopeless or incurable because Christians have the power in numbers to change our country's collision course. But we Christians must wake up in our pews and start voting for those who hate corruption and will lead America steadily back toward a righteous path and ultimately to God. Jesus said, *"What will it profit a man if he shall gain the world, and lose his own soul?"*

Christianity is a religion of fellowship and it is the greatest organization upon Earth. It is the most thrilling experience to know Christ and find comfort and reassurance in life and love. Every congregation in America must remain faithful and keep God's commandments above the laws of man. We must all realize we come into life with empty hands and we will leave with empty hands. Do not allow yourself to become a slave of wealth.

Even though some thoughts I have presented here are of a somewhat negative nature, as a Christian I do have a sense of true optimism and a divine revelation that if Christians will just wake up, everything will turn out well for our nation. **But we cannot continue to live like hell and expect Heaven to happen!**

It is a special privilege to have divine wisdom and continual guidance with Christ in our lives. Even as storms rage around us, with Christ in our hearts we can relax knowing we can have peace with God. Talk to God, commune with God, have a conversation with God, have some religion with God, have a relationship with God. Rest in this knowledge. May God bless each and everyone of you who are reading these passages as it is my hope you will find peace and understanding regarding God, Bible and Country.

Also by David L. Mundine

Behind The Glass Door

In 1965, at age thirteen, David's ordinary life was shaken by an extraordinary experience. This marked the beginning of many such experiences that he seldom shared for fear of ridicule. To write **Behind The Glass Door,** David Mundine had to overcome this fear of ridicule and humiliation.

After years of resistance he finally shares all the details of the visions and other deeply moving experiences of his life. It's a journey from which all of us can learn and gain inspiration.

Behind The Glass Door is now available at:

http://behindtheglassdoor.billspositivebooks.com/

Also available from Amazon.com and other book sellers.

Now also available as a beautiful, case laminate hardcover that makes a great gift.

www.ingramcontent.com/pod-product-compliance
Lightning Source LLC
Chambersburg PA
CBHW052055110526
44591CB00013B/2218